I WISH MY DAD TOLD ME THAT!

A PROGRESSIVE DATING GUIDE FOR YOUNG WOMEN

Irv Childress

authorHOUSE®

AuthorHouse™
1663 Liberty Drive, Suite 200
Bloomington, IN 47403
www.authorhouse.com
Phone: 1-800-839-8640

First published by AuthorHouse 2/21/2008

ISBN: 978-1-4343-5226-2 (sc)

Library of Congress Control Number: 2007909407

Printed in the United States of America
Bloomington, Indiana

This book is printed on acid-free paper.

Portrait by: Pat Rubin
               P.M. Studios
               1021 Amboy Ave
               Edison, NJ 08837

www.irvchildress.com

DEDICATION

This book is dedicated to all of the women in my life: my wife & two daughters, mother, mother-in-law, sisters, aunts, cousins and grandmother. A few had a lifetime of love. Others loved and lost. Some haven't begun to look for love. Some have hopeful prospects. Many are still waiting for "Mr. Right." A few are not looking anymore. My prayer for them all is that love and happiness finds them.

Contents

The Story

Dear Dr. Bob,

"My name is Bernard and I'm 28. Last month, I went to the car dealer; because I wanted to test drive the new *S2R*.

The car salesman took a glance at me in my new tweed sports jacket and super clean white button down dress shirt and did not hesitate to fulfill my desire to drive the car. He seemed more excited about the test drive than me.

When we got out on the two lane highway, the salesman egged me on.

'Don't you want to see what it can do?' He pushed.

'Certainly,' I replied. After all it was my third test drive of the week.

I was amazed by the car's cornering ability and gutsy get up and go. The auto's flashing and flickering indicator lamps kept my eyes darting to and fro across the dashboard. I got a warm and fuzzy feeling in my chest from the car's great agility. My ears flared backwards and the sensation of cool creamy vanilla custard ice cream sliding down my neck filled my body, as I cruised down the road at 70 miles per hour.

After I stopped at a traffic light, I glanced over to the driver in the left lane. He was driving a *Vulture*. He looked at me over his sunglasses and nodded. I looked at him and nodded in agreement. Then I noticed his car twist-rocking from him mashing the accelerator pedal. I revved the S2R's engine with confidence. 'Yeah, it's on,' I thought.

My heart pumped with an accelerated beat. My fingers tingled with excitement as I waited for the light to change.

The salesman chuckled and said, 'go for it!'

The light changed and we peeled out. Ten seconds later, I glanced at the speedometer and the needle was resting on the 90 miles per hour spot.

'That was quick,' I thought, as my heart played a new tune on my rib cage.

The *Vulture* driver had me by two car lengths, when it happened.

An overstuffed garbage truck pulled out in front of me as I neared the small intersection. As the truck slowly cleared the intersection, I swerved and missed the rear of the garbage truck. For a split second, I lost control of the vehicle and swerved back and forth. I looked to my right to see a telephone pole getting extremely close to the car's path. I scrambled to regain control, but it was too late. The vehicle had its own inevitable course and scraped the pole before I could regain control.

I pulled over on the shoulder. I felt my heart drop and it was banging up against my navel. After a brief pause, one bead of sweat ran down my left temple. I peeled my hands from the steering wheel. I unbuckled my belt to examine the car's damage.

But first, I had to make sure my sphincter muscle didn't fail me.

Everything was A-OK in my underwear. So, I got out of the car and ran around to the passenger side.

While I ran around the rear of the vehicle, the salesman struggled to open his door.

'Bang!'

That was the sound the door made, as he opened the mashed door.

'This is just terrific,' the salesman wailed in sarcasm.

As he opened the door, the passenger window shattered into billions of pieces.

'Ouch!' the salesman yelled. 'I cut my finger on the glass.'

As I watched the blood trickle down his ring and pinky fingers, I shook in my pants. I felt a couple of drops of nervous pee squeeze out.

'I hope that pee doesn't show up on my designer blue denim pants,' I thought.

My mouth hit the asphalt when I gazed at the enormous dent in the passenger door.

'I shouldn't have taken the ride,' I lamented from within. 'My auto insurance lapsed last week.'

I had no intentions or ability to purchase the car. I couldn't afford a $50,000 *S2R*. Man, my mom had to help me with my cell phone bill last month. Needless to say, the car was way out of my reach. I was only behind the wheel for the fun of it.'

'I hope you have the money to pay for that,' the salesman said with great concern.

As I looked at the dent with great uneasiness, my heart skipped a couple of beats and my rib cage was getting tighter. I wasn't surprised to see that the one bead of sweat on my temple turned into thirty.

'How am I ever going to pay for that?' I thought.

'My insurance should cover it,' I blatantly lied to the salesman.

'I'm driving us back to the car lot,' the salesman said with indignation in his voice.

When we arrived back at the dealership, I handed the salesman the bogus insurance card I kept in my *'92 Ford Escort.*

I went home and told my Momma what happened. She screamed at me and told me, 'I'm not going to fix this one.'

Everyday, the salesman calls my home asking for money. He wants money for the repairs to the vehicle. He wants money for his medical bill. And he wants an extra two thousand dollars for loss of vehicle use.

Although I gave the salesman the name of my insurance company, he continued to call when he found out that I wasn't insured. I only wanted to test drive the car. Who would've thought that I'd have an accident while on a test drive? I don't have the money to pay for the damages or the loss of use. He's threatening to take me to court. What can I do?"

Dear Bernard,

"You should have put more thought into your actions. If you knew you weren't ready to accept responsibility for the vehicle and his lacerated fingers, you should have never gotten behind the wheel. Here's my advice to you. Make the best of the situation. Be a responsible man and own up to your mistake. Get a second job. Make arrangements with the dealer to pay for the damages you've caused."

How did we get where we are?

In this story, Bernard knew he wasn't ready to make a commitment to the *S2R* with a finalized purchase. However, he drove it anyway.

It's a shame to admit it, but this is the approach that most men take in their relationships with women. This approach, most likely, has been going on since the beginning of time. But only in the last thirty five plus years has it reached epidemic proportions. Now, more than ever, young Black American women are being test driven by young Black American men, and when accidents or consequences occur, most of the men are not prepared to man-up and accept responsibility for their actions.

The end result from the irresponsible actions of men is an increasing epidemic in our communities. Many Black American women, over the age of 34-1/2, will never marry.

As a whole, the marriage rate in America is declining. It was recently discovered that married couples no longer have the majority in regards to coupled relationships in the United States.

If you're a Black woman over the age of thirty, you're 25 percent less likely to ever marry compared to white women of the same age. *(African American Marriage Patterns, Douglas J. Besharov & Andrew West, Hover Press)*

In 1963 when Dr. Martin Luther King Jr. gave his *"I Have a Dream"* speech, more than 70 percent of all Black families were headed by married couples. In 2002 that number was 48 percent. *(The Shocking State of Black Marriage: Experts Say Many Will Never Get Married, Ebony, Nov 2003, by Joy Bennett Kinnon)*

In the period from 1950 to 1997, premarital births grew to nearly seventy percent in the Black American communities. That's a fourfold increase from the 1950 figure of eighteen percent. This increase isn't because of an explosion of births outside of marriage. This fourfold increase represents the fact that we're still having children, but marriage is no longer a prerequisite. *(African American Marriage Patterns, Douglas J. Besharov & Andrew West, Hover Press)*

Over the past 35 years, the number of women over the age of 34-1/2 and never been married has steadily increased.

To get to the root of our marital problems, we must go back in time—back to the years of pre and post-segregation. That's where the shifting in the marital status for Black America began.

It's quite obvious that in the 40's and 50's, pre-marital sex existed. However, women or girls that engaged in premarital sex were stigmatized and were a shame to their families.

During that same period in history, it was even more of a disgrace for a teen girl or woman to have a child with no one to call "husband."

In the 40's Dr. Kinsey introduced sexuality to America. He taught on the different stages of sexual arousal for men and women. He also talked about taboo sex—men with men and women with women.

I believe Dr. Kinsey's greatest accomplishment was teaching men and women to understand the fundamentals of sex and to get men and women talking about sex. Communication about sex (in the context of marriage) can help couples achieve great sexual satisfaction.

Dr. Kinsey's discoveries were not all positive. When single or non-married men and women began to openly talk about sex, the spirit of promiscuity slowly escaped the genie's bottle and we've never been able to push it back in.

Although a few daring people began experimenting with sex, the fear of pre-marital pregnancy kept most legs closed.

But then, in the early 60's, an invention called "the pill," was the key driving force in limiting the amount of unwanted pregnancies. At the pill's beginning, it was only offered to married people. In 1972, the genie's bottle opened even further and single women were allowed access to the pill.

Premarital sex increased among single women as fear of unwanted pregnancy became almost nil.

Let's look at some down home history. If you were a young 1940's or 1950's girl and found yourself unwed and pregnant from a man that skipped town, you'd disappear into a far corner of the country, live with a family relative and have your child. When and if you returned, many times to keep the family honor, Grandma (your mother) assumed the role of Momma. A whole host of lies was told to keep the family name unscathed. Even with the lies, most of the time the truth was still known by everyone in your immediate circle. They just acted like the shame didn't exist—while they were in your face. Oh, but behind your back, the gossip swirled endlessly.

Some families didn't bother to tell the lies. They just threw the girl out on the streets.

If the pregnant girl's daddy knew where to find the boy that soiled his daughter, a shotgun wedding was in order. And the boy better not stutter when it was his turn to say, "I do."

In the 60's, the sexual revolution popped on the scene, and at the time it didn't matter much to Black people. We were in a social battle with our beloved Dr. Martin Luther King leading the way with power and might. Even though we didn't care about the sexual revolution at its coming out party, the revolution would influence Black America in the '70's and '80's.

The sexual revolution bolstered strength in the 1960's. However at the same time, seventy percent of homes in Black America were still headed by married couples. Why? When we as Black America found ourselves in the struggle to dismantle segregation, it left little time for us to run around with signs and holler, "free love" and "peace & love." We wholeheartedly needed to be equals with white America. It's not easy to take on the America's and/or the world's problems from the position of oppression. It's not easy to be influenced by the world while in a fight for equality.

The 1960's provided a host of social changes. Along with "the pill," the sexual revolution, and desegregation, social welfare programs were born.

The Federal government's programs assisted in the way we, as Black Americans, feel and act in regards to our marital habits, and offspring, as many of the new social programs were not conducive for marriage.

In June of 1963, the Federal government had its hand in social reform. The United States Supreme Court decided (8 to 1) that Bible reading and prayer in public schools were unconstitutional. At the time of the decision, eighty percent of Americans disapproved of the verdict. But much to the majorities' dismay, the verdict was permanent.

Since it's beginning, the United States of America utilized the Bible for many of its founding decisions. The Bible was the moral compass in America. Our founding laws are based on Biblical principles and truths.

If you are ever in the Washington D.C. area, take a tour of our governing buildings. The congressional building has tablets of the "Ten Commandments" at the top of the stairs leading into the building. Sculptures of Moses holding the "Ten Commandments" are commonplace in the building.

I bet the founding fathers of this country never envisioned that their foundation and plans for the future of this country would be challenged and overturned in the same court system a hundred eighty seven years later.

The guiding compass of life (the Bible) was declared unconstitutional and removed from daily study in schools.

I'm from the era of no Bible in school. I started school in 1971—eight years after the Supreme Court ruling. We never picked up the "Word of God" in class. I never saw a Bible on the teacher's desk. No one had ever read a passage of scripture in class.

During my school years, I cannot say that I wished that the Bible was in school. As a child, I was glad that one area of my life didn't include any attributes of church.

However, during my years of public schooling, I witnessed a yearly great moral decline. In 1984, on my graduation day—while we were sitting out on the football field waiting for our names to be called, I smelled weed burning. Yeah, some of my fellow classmates couldn't wait to get to the party before getting high. What a way to begin life as an adult. I bet the graduating class of 1971 would've never dreamt of smoking weed on the graduation turf.

I've recognized something about prayer and Bible reading in school. Even if a person is not a total believer of the words in the Bible and Jesus Christ, something is released in the atmosphere when the words from the Bible are read orally. The peace of God is released in the atmosphere. Human consciousness of right and wrong are developed. And even though a man or a woman might do wrong—they know beyond the shadow of a doubt that they are doing wrong, because of the moral compass that was being calibrated daily by the Word of God.

In earlier Bible reading days, man and/or woman were clearly aware that their current course of actions was Biblically wrong or correct. In other words, the people in the 40's & 50's knew the right thing to do, and they knew when they were doing the wrong thing. They were well informed sinners. He or she is well informed of the decision at hand and the soon to be consequences.

Nowadays, because the compass (the Bible) is no longer setting precedent for morality in most of our school systems, we have several generations of men, women, boys and girls making decisions and have no consciousness of what the Bible says about those decisions and what the possible consequences will be.

It's sad, because only one side of the moral ruler is being taught, "If it feels good—do it." In time, we all learn that "doing whatever" costs a whole lot more than anyone will openly admit. Sometimes "*doing whatever*" can cost you your life.

What does the removal of the Bible from public school have to do with the marriage rate among Americans? It has a great deal to do with the decline of the marriage rate. The Bible teaches of marriage being "*honorable in all.*" In other words, God honors marriage. One of the benefits of marriage is frequent love making. Outside of marriage, all sex comes with consequences.

With the Bible being read and taught on a daily basis in our school systems across America, morals or limits are developed—even inside the people that did not want to follow its teachings.

Without the Bible, men and women are left to create rules that agree with what he or she thinks is right at the time.

In the absence of law, there's lawlessness. The same is true in regards to morality.

The Bible says, *"Man does not live by bread alone, but on every word that comes from the mouth of God."* ***Matt. 4:4***

There are two worlds in which we live—one of the Spirit and the second of the physical or natural. In current events, many Americans deny the spirit factor in which our fore-fathers were so conscious of.

Cater to the physical world and you'll reap the benefits of living a life full of physical or carnal desires. The Bible says that you'll reap death. I submit to you that the death here is throughout life and most times can lead up to physical death (quick or slow).

Living a life after the flesh can kill a marriage. Living a life after flesh can make your children want nothing to do with you. Living a life after the flesh can cause you to loose family members. Examine how you feel the next time the family drunk comes around.

Cater to the spirit world in Christ Jesus and you'll reap life—great marriage—moving towards your purpose and destiny—children that love the Lord and parents— just to name a few.

Jesus said, *"...I came that you might have life, and have it to the full"* (or fullest). ***John 10:10***

I say all of this to make the point—no one throws away the owner's manual for the new car they've just purchased. The manual (or Book) stays with the car until the end of the car's life. The "book" is used to guide in the maintenance processes, show what all the knobs and gadgets are for, and many times it will help with troubleshooting the warning light on the dashboard that won't go away.

The same is true for the Bible. The Bible is our life's manual. As a country, we have many warning lights on the dashboard, and we haven't taken the vehicle in for service since 1963. We are headed for some costly repairs.

It's time for us to pick up the owner's manual (Bible) and find out why those warning lights are "on" the dashboard. Not only that, it's time for us to pick up the Bible just to make sure the auto is operating like the manufacturer said it would. It's time for us to pick up the Bible and learn how to use the power seats, electric windows and the navigation system.

Remember our time in slavery and segregation? Most Black Americans took refuge in the church. We lived, ate and slept Bible at a time when most of us couldn't read or write and had every excuse to turn our backs on God.

In the 21st century, we are free to do just about what ever we want. We have more millionaires in the Black American society than ever before in our history. Look how we treat our God that saw us through slavery, segregation, and oppression.

During the late '60's and early '70's, unemployment among Black men skyrocketed to double digit percentiles. The welfare system designed by our governments to bring financial aid didn't allow our married unemployed fathers to live in the home legally.

The scene in the 1974 movie *Claudine* depicted a great summary of where it all began when Roop (James Earl Jones) couldn't be seen at his girlfriend's apartment when the social worker unexpectedly dropped by. Remember the scene in the movie when the children were hiding many of the appliances, because the social worker would question where the money came from to purchase the stuff?

The welfare systems of the time rewarded our mothers with more income for having children by the nowhere to be found Pappas.

Talk about being double minded. The government increased your financial benefits when you had children out of wedlock. Why didn't they ask where the daddy was and make him pay?

Without really taking notice, a new way or a new standard of living was slipped in on the Black American society by our beloved Federal government. When the government assumed the role as CFO (Chief Financial Officer) of our households, they began to dictate what our families should look like. In a roundabout way, they've compromised the Black American Family.

Think about it. Our country...America, was not supporting marriage for African Americans.

In addition to the government instituting programs to annihilate marriage in the Black community, the Black man of the '60's and '70's faced many other relevant obstacles. Racial tension and the previously mentioned unemployment were the most devastating to the Black man's patriarchal position.

Think about this. How would you feel if society treated you as an animal? In addition to the degraded social standards you lived by, the Black male of the time found it very difficult to get a job because of race and education limitations.

As a man of meager means, the only thing in this world of that is of real value to him is his family. It's hard to feel like and/or be a man in front of his family because he cannot adequately provide for them. And now because he's unemployed, being with his family can jeopardize its survival because of the much needed financial assistance received from the US of A. So, the man is forced to take public assistance because he can't feed his family.

The government allowed the Black woman of the home to receive assistance. Now that his wife is on public assistance the husband must leave in order for his family to receive full entitlement from the government. If he stayed at home legally, his occupation of the home cost his family money.

The sons and daughters of these Black men suffered the most from the government social policies of the '60's.

Sons were left to live life with out fathers. Our primary source for learning to be a man was no longer available.

Hats off to all of the mother/fathers out there, but boys need a strong male influence around them. If you don't think that's true, look at the rate that gangs are growing. One of the key recruitment points for gangs is brotherhood (got to belong to someone—got to mimic someone).

I suggest that you find some positive brothers to bring into your sons' lives. If positive interjection lacks in the lives of young males, they are left to fend for themselves. And when they do, because of being naïve, they will most times make big mistakes that can lead to incarceration.

Then we (as Black men in training) have to listen to our man-scorned mothers (divorced or unwed) claim, "you ain't no better than your father." We listen to our mothers teach our sisters not to rely on us. Without realizing it, some mothers with their fiery tongues have become worst than society and any marriage killing program the government can come up with.

Sure, girls need to learn to take care of themselves. But when teaching our girls to be self reliant, we need not destroy the self image of her brothers that are possibly listening in the other room.

If you've been scorned by a Black man (and almost every Black woman I've talked to has been), keep the hostility to yourself. When you need to vent about the crap that your man has done to you, vent in front of your peers—not in front of your children.

When we (Black men) become teenagers and young men, we struggle to find our manhood. Our fathers were not there to tell us or give examples of what a real heterosexual marital relationship looks like—much less what a man looks like.

As children and teens, many young Black men witnessed their mothers lying down with different men looking for love in all the wrong places.

We heard our peers tell us, "A true man has as many women as he can handle."

Now that we've heard our mothers telling our sisters, "don't rely on a man," we wonder (with lack luster confidence) how to conquer the Black female. No one has ever told us that the Black female is a human being—not some piece of meat to jump on, do your business and keep it moving. No one ever told us to treat your girlfriend just like you'd treat your mother and grandmother (with respect).

We (Black America) are just as much to blame as the American government. We've stopped watching where our families are heading, and slowly adapted to an anti-family way of living.

Now, forty plus years later, most of us are victims of the present day marital crisis.

Unbeknownst to us, the very principals Dr. King died for were slowly stolen from us, because we failed to watch where we were headed.

In the '60's, when Martin Luther King gave his speech, most of our families were headed by married couples. As I mentioned earlier, the '60's were tough times for African Americans. Black men were being lynched. Our women were being raped. The south was segregated. We worked for ½ and ¼ of the pay that whites received.

But even with all of the oppression, we maintained a seventy percent marriage rate. How was that possible? Somewhere along the times, we've lost our core values.

Now, in 2007, marriage is becoming an expensive and highly avoided commodity in our society.

Black men find themselves right at the bottom in the pot called troubles. We have women who claim that they don't need us. We have a society that still fears us. We have a government that desires to cage us.

On the flip side of the coin, Black men are not innocent. In a sense, the Black man has enslaved Black women. Have you looked at a music video lately? I don't see many white men degrading our women in our music videos. We do enough of that to ourselves.

Have you looked at the countless one-sided relationships (woman in charge—spiritually and financially)?

Deep inside, it is my belief that some Black men are envious of Black women, because of their will to prosper—even in adverse conditions. Nowadays, women are more educated, take more risks, and have the double indemnity rule going for them (Black and female). The only way we (Black men) feel in control (or feel like a man) of these upward bound women is to control the women in the bedroom.

After years of hearing our mothers tell our sisters not to trust a man, we've decided to play with your emotions—because most women are led by emotion.

These are the consequences we face when young men are left to their own concept of manhood and have no clue as to what manhood is all about.

Unless a brother is inspired by someone positive, his history will follow others.

Women, I submit to you that this is the past of the Black man in which you're hoping to marry. As you can see, it is a great undertaking.

Through the course of history, we have seen the Black family dismantled by external and internal forces. Let's not be part of the problem. Let's not further the generational curses. Let's be part of the solution. Let's change our own destinies by being responsible human beings.

I hope to bring clarity and understanding to our marital situation. It is my hope to bring marriage to life again. It is my utmost desire for men and women around the world to see that a good strong marriage is a helper—not a hindrance.

In the passages that follow, I hope to inform and educate on the way Black men and men in general think. I hope to teach you the ways of men.

Let's get started.

When is a man ready to marry?

Who are you dating? Boy or man?

Too many boys are perpetrating the good man's life. Just as the car salesman found out in the beginning of the book, it's too late to find out you're dating a boy six months into your pregnancy. It's too late to find out your new beau is a player after you've bumped uglies. It's too late to find out your man is a Momma's boy right after you've signed the lease to cohabitate. It's too late to find out your man doesn't believe in work, after the repo-man hooks your Beemer. It's too late to find out your man has distribution issues after you've been arrested for having a garden hidden in your basement.

You need not waste your time with these relationships. If you're ready to marry, you need to know what constitutes a ready man for marriage. This will help in avoiding the riff-raff and many of the unfortunate consequences of life.

It's amazing to me. Many boys are getting the privileges of responsible married men. Boys are allowed to have sex too early in the relationship—make babies and run—never accepting their part as responsible men and/or fathers. And the sad part about this truth is;

young single women are still rewarding boys with the privileges of responsible married men.

Just because a man has pubic hair, big muscles, a deep voice and a sperm count does not make him a man.

Too many men are lounging in the "preparation years" (13 to 26 years of age) when (if marriage is the goal) the men should be preparing for marriage.

When a man meets you at twenty six or twenty seven, he should have a few goals in life accomplished like; a decent occupation, a place to live and reliable transportation.

Upon your first encounter with the man, the two most important accomplishments of the three are occupation and living quarters. If you meet a man without these two accomplishments completed, he's unprepared for a marital relationship with you. His time to prepare was wasted. Don't allow the man a chance to prepare. He cannot meet you and begin to prepare for the opportunity. That's like getting a job as a tax accountant and never going to college for accounting. A tax disaster is inevitable.

Once he's met you, the big two (job and living quarters), at minimum, must already be accomplished. If he comes to you without any of the big two, at the risk of being redundant, I'll repeat myself. He's unprepared. And if you desire to marry, now is the time to tell him, "Git ta steppin." Don't even waste one of your monthly cycles on him.

I like to watch the *Discovery Channel*. I find nature fascinating. I enjoy watching the big cats on the Serengeti best (lions—tigers—cheetahs). The big cats' way of life intrigues me. How they survive through the dry seasons and the intense heat of summer is amazing.

Believe it or not—the big cats live by rules and codes. We can learn from some of these codes.

At the end of the first stage in a young male lion's life, he's kicked out of the pride around eighteen months to two years of age.

The male lion's wake-up call is quite rude. One day out of the blue, Mom and Dad show serious aggression towards the male lion. They want to let him know "time is up—GET OUT!"

Has your man been given the wake up call by his parent or parents? Sometimes love must be tough. How can a man ever discover the answers to real life questions living in Mommy's house?

After the wake-up call is given, the second stage of life begins quite abruptly. The young male lion must fend for himself quickly or face his inevitable death.

In the beginning of stage two the male struggles for survival. The beginnings of the struggle for survival are evident by the silhouette of rib bones advertised from within his fur coat. At this stage of his life, he eats what ever he can get his paws on. He'll eat rabbits, dead carcasses, mice, bugs, tortoises, and even small crocodiles or steal a meal from a hyena, cheetah or tiger.

After chasing and killing his prey many times, he can only hope at best to gobble down a few good chunks of meat before having his kill stolen by other nomad lions or hyenas.

Life in exile is a high contrast from life at home with Mommy and Daddy lion. When he was home with his Momma, he ate from the top of the food chain—zebras—gazelles—wildebeests—buffalos—young elephants and rhinos. Now he's forced to eat crap until he can provide better for himself.

Only the strong lions survive the second stage of life. In two to three short years, he must learn to hunt and defend himself successfully. This is, by far, the most challenging period in the life of a male lion. Need I remind you that the male lion learns to hunt on an empty stomach? An empty stomach is enough to motivate the lion to action.

The same principle applies with marriage. A horny man is more motivated to get down the aisle than one that has his physical needs met on a regular.

The early years of manhood (stage two) are the most critical time of a man's life. This is the time in life where he gets his continuing education or trade. After receiving his extended education (beyond a high school diploma), he begins his occupational journey to transform his dreams and aspirations into reality. Stage two separates the boys from the men.

It's also a great time for women to spot the slackers. If during the transformation stage the man isn't busy working to perfect his particular craft, it's best to drop him as a hopeful prospect. Why would you want a man that lacks motivation? Why would you want a man that has to be pushed along? The Bible says, *"A lazy one puts his hand into a dish, and he will not return it to his mouth."* **Proverbs 19:24** It's a sad case when a man doesn't have enough drive to make sure he's feeding himself. If a man doesn't have enough drive to nourish his own body, how will he ever feed and care for you? What a pitiful human being. Why would you consider marrying a man like this? Why would you give a man like this your body? Why would you give a man like this children?

I knew a lazy Christian man like this. Needless to say, after eleven years of marriage, he lost his wife and children. I believe this man was definitely given way too much time to get it together. At best, he should've gotten only three months of dating—*never marriage.*

The Bible says *"For even when we were with you, we commanded you this, that if anyone would not work, neither should he eat. For we hear that there are some who walk disorderly among you, not working at all, but being busybodies...* **2 Thessalonians 3:10-11**. If a man doesn't work, he doesn't deserve the privilege of eating. If he doesn't deserve the privilege of eating, sex should definitely be a "no brainer."

We all know what happens to people that don't eat. Eventually, they die. Dead men can't have sex.

Don't forget that male lion's meals are on foot and aren't walking up to him and asking, "Hey, did you eat today? Take me. I'll feed you."

Feeding the lion means the lion will have to be smarter and faster than its prey. Someone has to die for the lion to survive.

When a man takes charge of his destiny, sacrifices must be made. Some things have to die—boyhood.

It's highly probable that when you encounter your "Boo," he might not have his *Benz*. A man with direction and driving a hooptie is far better than a guy living at home with his Momma (driving a *Benz*) slinging rocks and bud from his bedroom window.

Also, during hunting, the lion must make sure he doesn't get injured by his meal. If he gets kicked in the wrong place—like the jaw or leg—that injury may not be fatal at the time, but it will be fatal eventually. One of the keys to the lion's survival is the ability to successfully hunt. If he can't run, he can't eat. If he can't tear flesh with his mouth, he will die eventually. You want a man that is skillful in bringing home the bacon. You want a man that has several legal channels for the bacon to move in his direction.

The young male lion is in his prime at about five years old. Hopefully, during his travels, he's found a partner (brother or male cousin) to aid in his success as a hunter. If he's made it this far, he's proved *himself* to *himself* (self-confident). He's aware of all of his enemies (unemployment, being taken advantage of, dead end position at work). He knows where to find water, food and shelter (has his own crib and is not receiving welfare from the government or his parents). He knows how to take care of himself.

"Husbands, love your wives, even as Christ also loved the church and gave Himself for it, that He might sanctify and cleanse it with the washing of water by the Word, that He might present it to Himself as the glorious church without spot or wrinkle or any such things, but that it should be holy and without blemish. So men ought to love their wives as their own bodies. He who loves his wife loves himself. For no man ever yet hated his own flesh, but nourishes and cherishes it, even as the Lord loves the church" **Ephesians 5:25-29**.

Once again, if he cannot take care of himself, how can he take care of you?

Now, after many *failures* and successes, it's time to find a pack of lionesses, so he can pass his genes on to the next generation (stage three).

Only the successful are allowed to mate.

At the proper time, when he's alone or he and his male partner come into another lion's territory, they're ready for battle. Yes, they have to earn their right to mate by proving stronger to the current powers that be.

A battle breaks out and the two younger male lions are successful in running off the older male lions from the pride.

The first thing on the agenda for the new regime is to kill all the young cubs. (Be careful of men with this mentality. You want someone to love you as well as the fruit of your loins. Never get involved with anyone that cannot accept your children from a previous relationship as their own. If you do, over time, that individual will kill your child (not literally). He will constantly remind the child that he or she does not belong to him. He will treat his biological children with favoritism. That is enough to kill any child's spirit.)

Yeah, that's sad—but highly necessary. Why? The new kings will only be in charge for two to five years. They can't waste time raising another lion's offspring. Besides, the female lions will never come into estrus (horny for cubs) while she's nursing the evicted male's cubs. The new king must get his gene pool started as soon as possible.

It's funny to me how man/boys are allowed to mate—when in the wild, nature doesn't allow young inexperienced male lions to just run up in any female lion and father cubs at will.

Elephants are another animal I like to watch. An elephant's life span is from 60 to 70 years. Yet, even though male bulls sexually mature at about 12 years of age, they don't have the opportunity to *fight* for a mating session until around age 20. Remember, I said fight.

Young elephant bulls live a solitary life, because— like the lions—they're kicked out of the group between the ages of 12 and 14.

During the prime mating years, the male elephant can smell the female elephant when she is in estrus. Trust me on this one. He's not the only one that can smell the call for loving. Usually, another male is already courting the female. A battle breaks out (not to the death of one of the bulls) and the most powerful bull gets to sire the next generation. And again, the elephant has experienced some of the same challenges that the lion has had prior to this battle.

Three reasons for stating this:

1. A good man will have left his parents' home (willingly or unwillingly)—willingly is preferred.

2. A good man will have proven to others (but most of all to *himself*) that he not only can take care of himself, but also a family.

3. Being highly confident in his ability to provide for himself and new up and coming family, now he's ready to compete for a relationship with you.

The Bible is very clear on these three things and nature reiterates it—time and time again. In the word of God it states: *"Therefore a man shall leave his mother and father, and cleave to his wife and they shall be one flesh."* **Genesis 2:24** God's plan is for man to grow and mature, marry, and bring children into that marriage to keep the human race moving forward.

A desirable man is one who has taken the time to educate himself in a trade or skill. It is during the nomad years (right after being thrown out of mommy and daddy's home) that he should be busy learning those skills.

A desirable man is one who knows when a season of his life is over. There is a time for a boy to be at home with Momma and Daddy—preferably when he's a boy. During this time he learns life's basics.

But when that time expires or that season passes, it's time for him to make his own way.

A man that cannot recognize when a season is over will always be too late—too late to make corrections in his relationships—too late to make corrections on his job—too late when making decisions concerning his purpose.

A man that wants to make his own way in life is the man for you.

I remember when I was looking to get married. On my twenty-fourth birthday, it hit me like a ton of bricks. I asked myself, "how long will you live with Momma?" I could make it on my own if I had to, but my mother was sickly. I was there to help her with the bills.

But something inside me snapped on my twenty-fourth birthday. It kept yanking on my heart, until I yielded to it. "It's time to go," the voice whispered over and over again. I had to leave.

I spent the better part of my twenty-fourth year on this earth trying to prepare my mother for my departure. Even with all of the thoughts of failure on my mom's behalf, I was still driven by the voice inside me to leave.

I know, it sounds cruel. But that's the way God designed it.

My mother lived her life. She had the opportunity to make her life be whatever she desired it to be, so I concluded in the end, "I need to live my life—mistakes and successes. Besides, what woman would want a twenty-four year old man living at home with his Momma?" What woman wants a man that's beyond thirty living at home with his Momma?

I believe a man, unless there are extenuating circumstances, should not be at home over the age of twenty-one. The man has got to be thrown to the wolves to see what he's got inside of him.

Intense heat from fire separates the impurities from gold. And so it is with men. Men need to be thrown into the fire for the refining process to be complete.

You see. We never know what's inside of us until external forces challenge our abilities. Pressure on a good man squeezes out what's inside of him (good potential).

A man living at home with Mommy and Daddy is still covered—protected—sheltered—shielded by their home. He will never build the self confidence he needs to lead his family living at home with his parents. When you're seeking a man, you're looking for a leader not a loaf of bread.

For example: Say you're married and it's the 27th of the month. The baby got sick and you dipped into the rent money for the doctor expenses. A confident man wouldn't cave under the pressure. He'd work the situation out somehow. After all, God designed men to be contributors or providers. A good man would find someway to make the rent on time, and he'll have enough pride and confidence in himself not to run backwards every time something goes wrong. In other words, he won't take the easy route and ask his parents, friend or relative for the money.

After a young man has been ejected from his parents' home, he'll be real busy trying to figure out the direction of his life. He doesn't need to be bogged down by the tangent pursuit of women. He doesn't need women throwing themselves at him.

It's during this time that you can find a true leader or a genuine husband.

Men's testosterone levels are at their peak from the mid teens until the mid thirties. Testosterone serves internal (motivational) and external (physical) purposes. Two of the internal purposes are listed below.

1. It drives men towards women.
2. It causes a man to have a certain amount of fearlessness.

There's a lot of misuse and abuse of testosterone. One of the biggest misuses of testosterone is the vain pursuit of women. If a man can demonstrate sexual self control during the early years of manhood, you've got a disciplined man. You can be assured that he will be a one woman man. One thing for certain, it is highly impossible that this man is the ever popular player or pimp.

"No man can ever control himself sexually," you're probably thinking. Yes, most men can control themselves sexually and will. They just have to be reeled back in.

Not all men *will* control themselves sexually, but the right type of woman can not only demand it, she can get it. If you're a woman that respects your mind body and soul, you won't have to demand respect. The respect will be given. Besides, men in the past have sexually respected women, and in times past, the marriage rate among Black Americans was much higher than it is now.

Men need the young years to get it together. If you get involved with a man before he's gained confidence in himself, purchase a good broom and dust pan, because, you'll need it for sweeping up the shattered pieces every time a great challenge comes along in his life.

There's nothing worse than to have a man that caves in every time a crisis appears. It's so outrageous to see a man tuck his tail like a dog and run off with fear leading him by the collar.

Once you find the man that has proven himself worthy to himself, parents and you, then it's time to date.

When you find this man, just as the man, you must be prepared for a relationship. Ladies, you need to be on top of your game. Why? He's on top of his. Don't be a woman with nothing to offer except your body—be a woman of essence—be a woman of wisdom—be a woman of virtue—be the best you that you can be.

Even when we (men) are in our sexual prime, we can spot a woman of dignity, class and elegance.

We, as men, do stupid things, but we are not stupid. When I was dating, I could tell in the first five minutes of conversation how long the relationship would last and what I wanted to accomplish by relationship's end.

Many, of the women that I chose to hang out with for physical reasons, were disgruntled with me at the end of the relationship and did vindictive things to me. (There's something about a woman scorned that can ruin weeks, months and possibly years of any man's life.)

Waiting for a guy to complete stage two or meeting a guy long after stage two has been accomplished is the best move you can make for the foundation of your marital relationship.

When you meet a man at the end of stage two, the need to parent this man has been eliminated. He's a full grown man, and most importantly, he knows it.

Men need a right of passage—to know when they've arrived or crossed over into manhood. After they've arrived, they need another good man to acknowledge his passage into manhood. That's why the fraternity brothers celebrate with a big ceremony when new pledges cross over. That's why Jewish people have bar mitzvahs.

A man needs to be respected as a man by the people in his immediate circle as well as the world at large. Countless women have met men before they start or even complete stage two. Stage two of a man's life is critical to all future accomplishments. He has to know that he can tackle any task and challenge without the assistance of his parents, girlfriend, wife, etc.

God has designed women to be help meets. She is to assist her husband in getting the Lord's will for his life accomplished.

Many women find themselves in the position of provider (man's position) all because the man has never completed stage two. These relationships are in serious trouble because, unfortunately, men are creatures of habit. If you rescue him once from a disaster, you'll have to bail him out again. After you've bailed him out five or six times, sadly it becomes a way of life for the man.

Ask any woman that has taken back a repeated cheating boyfriend or spouse. If you holler and scream the first time he does it, but readily take him back, trust me, most likely, he'll be back in someone's foreign bed again.

The code men live by

In order to get a man to understand where you're coming from, you must first speak his language.

If you want to know how to get in the marrying arena, you must first understand some things.

If you moved from the United States to France, some changes would be necessary. The first significant change to take place is the language that you speak. French is the language spoken in France—not English. In order to communicate effectively, you must learn French or bring an interpreter everywhere you go. Given that situation, I think I'd be inclined to learn French.

The same rule applies to men. Our foreign language of choice is respect. Men live by respect. Respect is our code.

Look back over history and you'll see each and every war was fought over respect or the lack of respect. In the '90's Saddam Hussein ran down to Kuwait and took over the country. He pillaged their women, killed the men and took over the oil fields. Back in 1941, the Japanese gave the United States the ultimate early morning dis. Hitler believed in a superior race and tried to force that way of thinking on the world. Hitler tried to rid the world of Jews. That's disrespectfulness at its best.

You don't need world events to see examples of respect or disrespect. In the 'hood, how many times has there been a beef because some other brother looked at his girl the wrong way? The lack of respect is most times at the root of most altercations.

I remember a couple of years ago when an NBA basketball player ran up into the stands to beat a man for throwing beer on him. That was the ultimate DIS-respectfulness on the fan's behalf. Of course, we all remember the controversy that followed.

If wars, gang bangs, fist fights and other various altercations are started because of dis-RESPECT, don't you think you ought to understand manly respect?

"But also let everyone of you in particular so love his wife even as himself, and the wife that she defers (respects) to her husband." **Ephesians 5:33**

I find this remarkable. Long before I began reading the Bible or was even born, respect, between husbands and wives, was already discussed. Note that the Bible instructs the man to love his wife, but doesn't tell his wife to love her husband. It tells her to respect him. Why? Most women are naturally given to love and affection. That's the core of women—love. If women were not given to love and affection naturally, how can they nurture the next generation? The world needs the love (especially motherly love) that women have.

More effort is required for a woman to respect a man than to love a man. As I stated earlier, "women are naturally given to love." Respect takes work.

It is a lovely thing to see a woman respecting a man. It is even more of a lovely thing to see a man that can be respected.

My grandmother was my symbol of womanly respect. During my time as a child, I never saw her disrespect my grandfather.

My grandmother and grandfather were an old school couple. My grandfather didn't cook, clean up the house, etc. My grandmother worked and kept the house clean. I can only remember her raising her voice to him on one occasion. She never talked negatively about him in public or to anyone else in her circle. And she had good reason to be disrespectful, because my grandfather was a bit of a player back in his day.

In my opinion, there's nothing worst than a disrespectful woman. I've seen many a woman yell at grown men just as if her husband or boyfriend passed through her womb. I've seen women cheat on their husbands and fleece joint bank accounts. I haven't seen it all, but I've seen enough disrespect to last a lifetime.

So it is with man. Not only do we understand respect, we live by it.

Think about our president George W. Bush II for a moment. Now, we've all got our opinions of him. But just for a moment, imagine George Bush in a chauffeur's suit and cap holding the limousine door open for you to enter the vehicle. Regardless of your opinion of the President of the United States, that's a disturbing site. (No disrespect to any chauffeurs out there. This is just an analogy.) President Bush has a certain place in all of our minds. It's an elevated place. He is to be served. He's not a servant. After all, he's the President of one of the most powerful countries in the world. How can President Bush stand there holding the door for me?

It might hurt some of you to say it, but George Bush II has a place of respect in the minds of every American.

So it is with women. Your first impression on a man's mind must be more than the obvious. Oh, we're going to check out your body and face. You can take that to the bank. I don't care if you're wearing thick brown stockings or the tiniest mini skirt. (By the way, short skirts are a way to get attention—just not respectful attention.)

Respect for yourself must emanate from your being. You must make the guy move to the second thought. What's the first thought? "How can I peel those panties?

How can I get her to share the brownie with me?" The second thought is: "she doesn't look like the type to be easy. Maybe this can go somewhere. Maybe she's the 'one.'" (Remember, this is for the guy you meet that is ready to marry. If he's not ready for marriage, the first thought will prevail. "How can I get her to peel the panties?") Once he has the second thought, you're starting to speak a language he can understand.

I often visit the supermarket. And the clutter of magazines near the register make me chuckle. *"Five new sexual positions he'll go crazy for" "Eight steps to get him to pop the question" "Are you in a Dead End relationship?"* These are some of the hook lines used to get you to purchase the magazines. What's the funniest part? Most of these articles are written for women by women. I often wondered how it's possible for women to tell other women how to catch a man, when they lack the greatest perspective of all. They are women—not men.

Would you go to the Chevrolet dealer to get your Mercedes repaired? Would you ask a homeless person to instruct you on financial matters? Yet, magazines are being sold by the millions on the premise of good advice—from other women.

There are many things that are most important when you begin dating. One of the first things you must do is command your level of respect. One of the ways new respect is established is by the way you dress. If you can't bend over without anything falling out or pushing through, there's a very good chance that you're not going to command much respect from a man. After all, hidden inside all men is animal instinct. And when you dress your person in a self disrespecting manor, it's almost impossible for him to turn off the dog and think like a civilized human being.

Let's face it. You are what you advertise. Don't ask, "Why are men only interested in my body and getting into the bedroom?" When, you have all of your body parts on display in the store window.

Don't get me wrong, I'm not telling you to dress in taupe stockings and an old maid dress. If you wear that stuff, you'll be lucky if an ugly man gives you a second look.

There is a respectful way to entice a man and bring him back to the discussion table. When you're getting to know each other, establish your rules (or in other words—respect boundaries) upfront. Be someone that he MUST respect!

Wear respectable clothing. And always have a neat and clean appearance. Keep your apartment or home neat and clean.

Keep your language free from profanity. I remember I dated this girl back in the '90's. Every other word out of her mouth was profane and vulgar. She came over for Thanksgiving dinner and was cursing like a sailor in front of my mother, even though, I didn't curse in front of my mother. She cursed like the ex-sailor that she was. I was appalled, but I didn't say anything. I just stopped dating her.

Ask your man politely not to use profanity around you. And make sure he knows that under no circumstances are you to be called any other name but the name given to you at birth.

Never ever treat your man like a son in public or private, even when he does the most detestable thing. I've seen men that have had their masculinity handed back to them after it was pushed through a meat grinder by their girl or wife.

Each man has space in his mind for the women that he respects (i.e. mother—grandmother). You want to enter that space.

Testosterone is a powerful narcotic. Once you've released too much testosterone in your new beau's body from revealing clothing, physical touches and/or dirty talking, it's hard to bring back sane thinking on his behalf. He will want to tear your clothes off each time he encounters you.

Respect must be established and maintained from the first time the man lays eyes on you. And from there, you can develop a deeper respect from him.

It is easier to dismantle respect than to build it.

Many women will sleep with a guy that once respected her and now because panty peeling was easier than expected, he's moving on.

I hate to keep referring back to the President, but during the first few weeks following September 11th, 2001, Mr. Bush had the highest respect achievable from the entire nation. His approval ratings were at an all time high.

Well, as the years progressed and a few misinformed decisions later, his approval ratings along with his respect dropped into the basement.

When you first meet the man, you must lay down your rules as soon and respectfully as possible.

When you are looking to marry, sex is not the most important aspect of the relationship. If that were true, you would've married the man that had you drooling like a little baby in the bed. Right? Of course, if you're honest with yourself, some other issue that was bigger than sex caused the relationship to sour like twenty day old milk.

In the past, I thought that "good sex" was the foundation for a good relationship. And after having a few good physical relationships, I soon discovered that good sex wasn't as important as I thought it was.

Respect, trust, friendship and love are the key ingredients to a great relationship. These ingredients make the sex fun, exciting and off the charts.

If you're fighting all the time after you've finished making love, what kind of relationship is that?

Besides, once you jump in the sack and the desserts are good, your judgment is now clouded. The "good sex" factor will have an unfair advantage in the decision making process, thus complicating a hard decision.

At the root of the "good sex" factor is fear. "I may not ever get satisfied like this again with someone else."

Clouded judgment or good sex before its appropriate time will make you stay in a bad relationship longer than expected, especially if new children are involved.

I cannot tell you how many times I should've heeded the little voice inside me or the voice of another concerned female family member. But, nooo, I just had to have some of that brownie. And don't get me wrong, it was fun while the relationship was on the new, fresh and exciting side. But, ooohh, I learned about the two sides of a woman. On the other side, of the new and exciting, were hurt, bitterness, and vindictiveness to name a few.

Respect is a key building block in a new relationship. You must keep the respect building while at the same time building a lasting trusting friendship.

When a man is ready to marry, the first thing he looks for is a woman to respect (someone like his mother). If you sleep with him on the first, second, third, fourth date, your chances of being considered for a long term relationship (although it does happen) are slim to none.

Believe it or not, when men are ready to marry, they're still looking for a "virgin."

There is also an old saying, "A man wants a lady in the streets—a mother to his children—and a freak in the bedroom." Notice the first quality of the ideal wife "A lady in the streets." His woman is a lady of respect. No one has been pillaging through her bedroom like Grand Central Station. People in the community have respect for her.

The "mother to his children" is a woman of great nurturing love.

The "freak in the bedroom" is the woman of his sexual fantasies. In other words, he wants her to do things behind closed doors that she can't tell her sister, best friend or Momma.

Immediately after you've gained his respect, you must gain his trust. I'll say this as simple as I can. If a man does not feel that he can trust you, he'll never commit to you.

We (men) want to know, "can we trust you?" Can we trust you with our finances? Can we trust you with marital fidelity? Can we trust you to help run the home? Can we trust you to honor our dreams and help make them a reality on this earth? Can we trust you to raise our children? And last but most important, can we trust you with our ego and emotions? Once I surrender my trust to you, will you treat it like a chest full of gold, or will you treat it like toilet paper?

If you ever want to bring a man down, gain his trust and then do something to destroy it.

I believe the number one reason why some men are not monogamous is the fear of trusting one woman with their sexual appetite.

Trust is more important to a man than a woman. I know you have got to be wondering, "How is that possible when men are the biggest abusers of trust?"

Oh, it's the truth.

When a woman cheats on her husband, it's highly unlikely (but not impossible) that the relationship will survive, because the man will have to learn to trust his spouse again. At this stage of the game (infidelity), many men will elect to start over with someone else, or not even bother with women at all.

I've had my heart busted up a few times and I've seen men with broken hearts. I can honestly say that trust in a relationship must be established long before "good sex."

Good single men are always looking for a trustworthy woman. A good single man is looking for a woman that will be with him in good and bad times. He wants to know that he can trust her to have his back in the event of a crisis—or even in stable times.

Good single men are looking for women of integrity—at work when she says that she's at work—spent the money where it was supposed to be spent—and truly honest with her thoughts, feelings and character.

Always be where you say you'll be. Never give place to doubt or distrust.

Find new appropriate friends—like another dating couple. Never have a lot of male friends. That is a recipe for disaster—even if it is strictly platonic.

Trust me. If you have a lot of male friends, the thought has crossed one of the fellas minds, "I wonder if she'll let me?" Your man understands this question all too well, because he's asked himself the same question in regards to some of his female friends.

Be a woman of your word. Always do what you say you're going to do. Never open the door for anti-trust. Please be consistent.

Once a man realizes that you are a woman of respect—not only do you command a certain amount of respect—you give respect to which respect is due. Then, he's pretty certain that he can trust you not only with his character, but his emotions and thoughts too, and then he is ready to move to the next stage—love.

An "in love" man can happen within a year's time. That is if and only if he's ready to marry.

If he's not ready to marry, you'll get stuck in the trust phase.

Men have two levels of trust. A jump off gets minimal trust. Wife material gets an upper level of trust. Most jump offs don't get to see the checking account balance. The future wife will.

Many women are not successful in moving from the trust stage to the love stage. Why? By the trust stage, sex is already on and poppin'. At the beginning of the relationship, the man was driving the relationships through the phases. Now that he's getting sex, his motivation to move the relationship towards love and then marriage has decreased. Only the guys really ready to marry will continue to push the relationship forward.

Many women spend the best years of their lives unsuccessfully trying to move past the trust phase in their current relationship. They've watched other girlfriends meet, date and marry all while waiting for someone to throw a hot pot of coffee on their man and awaken him from his stupor.

Moving from trust to love and then marriage is risky. The "fear of loosing what I got" kicks into overdrive.

Honestly, no woman or man wants to walk away from a relationship that has a seventy percent chance of sharing nuptials. But sometimes, you've got to do what you've got to do. While you're wasting your time with mister seventy percent, mister one hundred percent will never have the opportunity to appear.

In between trust and love is where the relationship needs a Chess move if you will.

You'll never force a man to marry you, so don't go there with conversation and/or making babies.

As men we need time to think and analyze the situation. Threats and tears will only work for a little while. In fact, threats can make us call your bluff, and you could possibly wind up being the odd (wo) man out.

Express how you feel to your man—about the relationship—what you want from the relationship— what the future entails with him, and invite him to be a part of it. Make sure you give him some time to think about the offer without any further interference from you.

During his time of pondering, make yourself scarce.

Don't be afraid. If he doesn't come to find you, he was never yours. You were wasting your valuable time with him.

Before making your Chess move it is important to avoid sexual contact. In fact, I hate to sound like a broken record, but sex obligates the parties involved. If no desserts were shared—no obligation and/or hurt will be felt. And if there is pain, the pain will come from the lost of a good friend.

When he does return, rest assured that he knows where the relationship is headed, and he'll continue to push in that direction.

The not so secret codes men live by

"Why buy the cow when the milk is free?"

"Why pay for the honey, when you can steal it from the bees? Of course, I might get stung a couple of times, but hey, it's free honey."

"Why should I purchase the car when I can go for a test drive at different dealerships on a monthly basis?"

"You gave me the cart. Now you want me to buy the horse?"

"You knew I couldn't afford the payments before you delivered the furniture. So why did you drop it off?"

"Awe baby, I love you. Just don't stop breaking off the brownie, because if you do, you'll get a real taste of my love."

"Since God formed Eve from one of Adam's ribs, I've got to keep me a few spare ribs around."

"I've got all the time in the world to get married. Shucks, I can have kids until the day I die."

The crazy things women think

Belief: If I don't give him some brownies, someone else will.

Truth: Someone else *will* give him some brownie. In fact, if you tell him, "NO brownie for you," you'll see how fast he moves on.

Actually, canceling the brownie supply is only for strong women only. It will take strength and perseverance not to return to supplying the brownies—especially if it was good. Why? Because, when you find out all he wanted from you was sex, your self esteem will take a slicing blow to its shins. Only the strong and disciplined women can recover from dessert cancellation, because the temptation to yield to the baseless thought, "I might as well be what men think I am," could drive you to bend and compromise your position.

Realize this. If you don't give him some brownie, someone else will. That is a fact of life. Most likely, you're a bus stop on his route. If there are no passengers to pick up at the stop, he's moving on to the next stop. He'll just be a little early for his next victim passenger. Let someone else have the trouble.

Belief: If I turn the bed upside down and keep him suspended in the air with my freaky ways, he'll see that he can't live without me. I'll freak my way down the matrimonial aisle.

Truth: As he's enjoying your freaky ways, he will simultaneously cast judgment on you. His primary thought will be, "I wonder how many other guys she has done this with?" Your chances of getting down the aisle with this guy are slim to none.

He's going to drink from your fountain until he's full or until you demand more than he's willing to give. Then he's moving on because the element of trust has been stretched.

Belief: "He says he's not ready for marriage, but I know he doesn't mean it."

Truth: Men are not that complicated. When we say we aren't ready for marriage, in truth we are saying, "I think there's someone out there that better suits me, but since you're breaking off brownies, I'm going to hang here until you either ditch me or someone better comes along." This relationship will be a time wasting effort on your behalf.

Let me share something with you. I always wanted to be married. I came from a broken home via divorce. You can read about those times in my first book, *Memoirs of a Broken Family* (ISBN: 1418454168). Even though I wanted to be married—and I was looking—I never let the women that didn't make the grade know that they would never be my wife.

Back in the day, I had a girlfriend that I reconsidered for marriage. The situation with this woman had some history. We dated a couple of years earlier. I had come to the conclusion after a few months of dating her (the first time we dated) that she was not the woman for me. However, we continued to date. All total, our relationship lasted over two years—off and on.

One day out of the blue, we had some direct discussions about our feelings towards each other. This was the beginning of the end of our first break-up.

Now let's set the record straight. I was not in this girl's dessert pantry. Honestly, I wasn't physically attracted to her. But she was really fun to hang out with. Both of us were dating other people while we occasionally dated each other, so it was a cool situation.

I stopped seeing her because we had gotten into a conversation about an important life factor. At the time I had strong beliefs in a happy marriage (money or no money). All she ever talked of was the fur coat she would own—the car she'd drive and the home she'd live in. I never heard anything about love or happiness flow from her lips. Love and happiness are very important to me. (Now don't try to say that love and happiness is what you're seeking with all fellas, because you'll soon be found out. Find your core values for a relationship and stick to them.)

Our break-up went like this: We scheduled a date one night. I had a habit of being late for the dates. We set the time for 7:30. She told me with a snarl in her voice, "be here at 7:25—not 7:45 or 8:00."

I don't like ultimatums, nor do I like bossy women, so I never showed up.

She called the house several times. My mother answered the phone and told her a few inconsistencies. (Yeah, she lied for me.)

She called the next day, and we had it out. She cussed me out. I have never been called so many mother/fathers in one sentence in my lifetime. At the end of the mother/father session, we were obviously letting the relationship go, and there were no tears or heaviness of heart.

I was elated to be out. I was elated that we never shared dessert, because that made the break-up simple. That was one of the easiest relationships that I'd ever walked away from. I owed her nothing, because I didn't obligate myself by having sex with her. If anything, she owed me for all the movies and dinners that I paid for.

She was lucky that I was willing to walk away from the money invested.

A few years later, I ran into her at the mall. We started talking and I decided to ask her out on a date.

By that time, I was in my mid-twenties and I was ready to cut out being a part-time player.

We dated frequently again. After about three or four dates, I remembered why I stopped dating her in the first place. She was too bossy and naggy.

And to make matters worse, after a few months of dating, she invited herself down to my apartment. I was hopeful and I thought my feelings might change if we shared dessert. So I let her come down.

Remember I told you that I wasn't physically attracted to her? Even though she was an overnight house guest, the sexual attraction never showed up and I wasn't about to ruin my reputation.

I wasn't attracted to her so I made no attempt to get things started.

The next day, I counted the hours to her departure. But first, I wasn't getting away with the past night's events so easily.

She went as far as to accuse me of being a homosexual.

Naturally, I had to fire back at the comment.

I was lying in my bed. She was heading towards the kitchen when I replied, "you're like a sister to me." Man...that was a *baaad* move. I heard a few of my newly purchased dishes slam into the bottom of the sink.

Well, we got into it.

I couldn't tell her the truth. She was bossy and naggy. Plus, I just wasn't physically attracted to her. How do you tell a woman *that* without hurting her feelings?

Later on in the day as I waited for the time to carry her fifty miles back to her home, we started to horse play a bit. The next thing I know, I'm struggling to keep myself from falling on her and possibly hurting her. I didn't fall on her, but my head slammed into my apartment door, and blood began to run down my face.

We went to the hospital and I received seven stitches above my right eye.

After we left the hospital, I tried to get her to go home, but now her maternal instinct kicked in and she wouldn't leave. She spent another night.

The next day she awakened with her virtue in tact.

I caught more grief because of my lack of drive.

I took her home later that day. Believe it or not, although she didn't verbalize it, she knew I wasn't coming back to see her anymore, so, on her way out of my car, she stole one of my favorite T-shirts that was laying in the backseat of my car. She knew, with my stolen T-shirt in her possession, she'd have one more opportunity to see me.

By the time I got around to meeting with her for the soul purpose of retrieving my T-shirt, I was dating my wife.

Once again at our meeting, the mother/fathers were hurled at me with lightning speed. I sat quietly and waited for it to be over, because I had already made my decision. I had a new girlfriend.

Ladies, listen to us. We don't know how to sugar coat things. We don't say one thing and mean another. Well, sometimes we do. But the truth is somewhere in that lack of response, brief response and/or the wordy response that you can't make any sense of.

Sometimes, we (men) don't know what we want or can't remember why we broke up with you in the first place. And we will waste your time until we figure it out again.

If you were to check any man's so-called "black book" (Today, it may be his *Palm, Blackberry, or Pocket PC.*), he might have all physical attributes and sexual tricks added to his entries. You'll never see an entry that states the reason for break-up. If you weren't really disrespectful to him, he'll get back in there and then and only then will he remember why it didn't work the first time.

I broke up with this girl. I made a decision and then revisited the decision.

Most men have no problems making a decision. Many times, we have a problem with informing you of the decision that's been made on your behalf.

As I stated earlier, when a man says he's not ready to get married, he's actually saying, "I think someone better is coming," or "I'm not finished raiding dessert pantries."

So now, a decision has been made on your behalf. Now, you have to make a decision, and if you decide to wait for him to get ready, I can assure you, it's a great possibility that you will not be his wife—even after waiting for him to get ready. Why not? If you're in a relationship with him while you're waiting for him to settle down, he will be participating in many other relationships. If you allow that, you're telling your man you have no regards for his respect towards you.

The key point here is to listen to what you are being told. Don't emotionalize it. Take it verbatim, until the man comes clean. When a man speaks from his heart, he'll have some difficulty doing it—especially when he thinks and feels good things about you.

If he says he's not ready for marriage, most likely he isn't. No amount of pressure, threats and ultimatums will allow the situation to move in your favor.

Put some time and distance between you and your man. See if he is really interested.

"No shows" are not interested. Take the hint.

Belief: I've got the best piece of brownie on this side of the Mississippi river. He'll never give this up.

Truth: If you're not the type of woman he's looking to marry and/or if he's not ready to get married, he's going to keep sampling the brownies. If your brownies are warm and chewy with the proper amount of walnuts, he's going to bring the whip cream, chocolate syrup, and vanilla ice cream.

However, the minute you run out of brownies, he'll take his part of the dessert and keep it moving.

Having the best piece of brownie will never get you married. And even if you're successful at having a man fall for you because of your infamous brownies, when he finds out that's all you have in common is dessert, he's going to book.

Good sex is a part of the foundation for a good marriage. Good sex was never meant to be the end all for a relationship.

Men, no matter how physically satisfying you are, are bound by this principal. A good man needs more than good sex, too.

Belief: Last night during dessert time, he told me he loved me. "He really loves me."

Truth: In the throws of passion, we'll say anything. "I love you," has been used by accident and abused many times over.

In the events leading up to orgasm, the brains of men are filled to the brim with a chemical called dopamine. When a man's brain is full of dopamine (the key word in dopamine is first syllable—dope), he's liable to give away all the cash in his wallet and bank accounts.

After the dessert bowls are washed and we return to our daily grinds, he's thinking, "I should've never told her, 'I love her.' What was I thinking?" Then the next time you talk, awkwardness and fear will be in charge. If he's not ready for a lasting relationship, this relationship will never recover from the powerful word blurted out in the throws of passion, unless someone is willing to settle for less than they deserve.

Never ever believe what you hear in the throws of passion.

Belief: He told me he wanted me to have his baby. If I have his baby, eventually, he'll marry me.

Truth: This is a short term decision with a long term casualty.

Most likely, he enjoys your brownies tremendously.

The young cats are good for this one, because they think that this is a pretty good way to secure your brownies for the future. Why do they think like that?

Inexperience—they don't believe they have what it takes to get another girl to share dessert with them.

Intoxication—you've really rocked their world.

Procreation—men have an innate desire to procreate. Sometimes, boys believe they are ready to be fathers before they've paid the financial bill of independence—like rent.

So the man *reasons* within himself and the *logical* solution to the above statements is, "If she has my baby, her brownies will always be on lock for me. When I stop by to see my kid, I can possibly get another piece of brownie.

She'll be less desired by other men, because she's the mother of my child (Remember how the male lion kills the cubs when he takes over the den? This is similar type of behavior—only in reverse)."

When you have this boy's baby, your maternal instincts will kick in and you will desire this boy to become a father and husband—or at least act like a husband.

That's a definite turn off for someone with a face full of pimples and not ready to be a dad—let alone a husband.

Believe it or not, the baby's and your needs will drive him into the arms of another childless woman—leaving you holding the bag—or in this case—the baby.

It's sad to say, but many girls find out what kind boy they're baby's daddy is when it's too late.

Throughout history and across all racial and ethnic lines, women have had babies for all sorts of reasons—gold digging, spitefulness, and/or as a form of control. What about the children? Would you want to be born in the middle of a parental war? If not, then plan accordingly. You have the power to control your destiny. Occupy your destiny.

New born babies deserve the opportunity to grow up with mommy and daddy living under the same roof as husband and wife. That does not always happen, but it is the best scenario for the children.

Belief: He says, "My wife and I are having troubles. It's not working out. As soon as the divorce is final, we can be together."

Truth: I've been married for over thirteen years. I've been on this planet for over forty years. I don't know of any marriage that's trouble free. I've never seen one. If you find one, please let me know. I'd like to stop by their house and take pictures, notes and situational recordings.

There is some truth to this statement. No marriage is ever "trouble free." A trouble free marriage is impossible. It will never happen so long as two imperfect people marry.

Have you ever met someone perfect in all his or her ways?

However, this is his wife and possibly children we're talking about. His wife made it through his testing grounds that you're now unsuccessfully treading in. Do you really think he's going to leave the mother of his children—the woman he chose to spend the rest of his life with for you?

Even if his marriage is really in trouble and he does decide to leave her, most likely, you will not be his first choice for remarriage. Why not? You've decided to get involved in a very disrespectful relationship. You're the "other woman." The "other woman" is not to be married.

The man may never verbalize this but he's thinking, "If she can be with me while I'm married, what else is she capable of?" or, "how do I know she won't cheat on me when we're married?" Men are so judgmental. Believe me; he has no respect for you in regards to the possibility of you becoming his wife. When you don't have a man's respect, you don't have one of the key elements that each man lives by.

Also, up until the time he possibly marries you, it will be all gravy baby. Think about it. Living with someone is totally different than sneaking around for dessert. Start asking the married man about where are we going to eat and sleep? Did you pay the cable bill? Did you pay the gas and electric bill? And take note of how often he comes to see you once you take the stance his wife now occupies. His place of escape (haven) has just turned into his home (the place of boring responsibilities), so he might as well go back home.

Belief: My chances for marriage are better if I live with him.

Truth: Apartments and leased cars have a beginning date and a termination date.

Leased cars have a date set for returning the vehicle at the conclusion of the lease. If you don't want to return the vehicle, they have a set price to pay. If you decide not to return the vehicle or make arrangements for the final payment, legally, they'll come and get it.

If you don't pay your rent, in the process of time you will be evicted.

You know when it's time to leave the apartment. You know when it's time to give the car back. The leases have a clear end date written on them.

When does the cohabitation contract expire? After you've wasted your prime marrying years with someone that has no intention on marrying you? After you've wasted three-quarters of your childbearing years in a dead end relationship?

Why would you live with a man without having signed the proper documentation (marriage certificate)? Why would you move in with a man and not have a contract?

The minute you move your things into the set dwelling quarters, you're whispering into the man's ear, "You don't have to buy this cow. The milk from this heifer is free."

It's too late to ask for a ring now, because you have lowered your standard. You've turned on the oven so he can have brownies at will.

Sure, it's fun in the beginning. Please tell me how fun it is when you've spent five or six years living with a man and the ticking from your biological clock keeps you awake at night.

Think about this. You'll never get what you really want if you compromise.

As a young boy in school, I struggled with geometry. The teacher never let up or slowed down the speed at which he taught the class. His answer for my problem, "I'm available after school if you need extra help."

My need for help was quite obvious. The big red "F's" on my test papers confirmed my need.

Eventually, after some strong belt-theology from Mom, I stayed after, and my geometry grades improved.

If the teacher had stopped teaching the class just to make sure I was getting it, I wouldn't have put any extra effort into learning geometry. "He'll make sure I understand it," would've been my prevailing thought and method of operation. The teacher would've extinguished my flame called drive.

The same thing happens when you move in with a fella. Most of the time, all motivation for the relationship to progress has ceased (especially if your man is from a home where marriage never existed or he's not ready to marry), because he's got plenty of milk, ice cream and brownies sleeping right next to him. Why should he really care how long this situation continues? He can have children all the way up until his death.

Ladies, never move in with a man that has no concept of marriage. If his mother and father never married and lived together for years, you must set the standard for your life and not live with him before marriage.

A man with no concept of married life will have difficulty understanding the benefits of marriage. He will see marriage as something to avoid. And you will be the primary avoidance.

Belief: I just met a new man. He said, "I'm the finest thing he's ever seen in his life. I can see myself spending a lot of time with you." Then he smiled and kissed my hand. I think I just met my future husband.

Truth: Most men that are not ready to get married will say something like this. The statement is very true. He can see himself spending a lot of time with you horizontally and any other pretzel moves he can get you into.

Men are hunters by nature. We get right to the point. Testosterone makes sure a man never forgets his primary purpose for being here on earth, *"And God blessed them. And God said to them, Be fruitful, and multiply and fill the earth..."* **Genesis 1:28** That was one of the commands God gave Adam. *"Be fruitful and multiply..."* As soon as Adam awakened from the deep sleep and took a gooood look at Eve, he said, *"This is now bone of my bone and flesh of my flesh. She shall be called Woman because she was taken out of man."* **Genesis 2:23** (I believe in my heart that when Adam saw the first woman ever in creation and in his lifetime and saw how fine she was, he struggled to compliment her. *"This is now bone of my bone and flesh of my flesh"* was the best he could come up with. Some things never change.)

I'd also like to take an educated guess and surmise, at that precise moment; testosterone began flowing through Adam's arteries and veins. Immediately following the onset of testosterone surge, he took a good look at her and then he felt and saw his own body reacting to what he saw. And Adam concluded within himself, "Thank you God!"

Of course, the Bible doesn't say it like that, but that's my spin on what happened when Adam saw the finest naked woman standing in front of him.

You see, Adam was physically attracted to Eve, because God made it so. God didn't want man to feel obligated to populate the earth. And believe me, no man does. In fact, we've bent the original plan of God so that we can get to the act of populating the earth without the populating part.

Testosterone ensures that no obligation on the man's behalf is felt. Men want to make copulation happen in the worst way.

Today as it was in the days of the first man and woman, the first step towards a relationship is still physical attraction. However in the latter 20th century and early 21st century, physical attraction has taken over as the primary reason for hooking up with someone sexually.

Another example of this is: Today, more importance is given to how much money a person makes at his or her occupation, instead of what a person does with the money earned. What a person does with earned money is more important than how much money the person makes. (If you make ten dollars per hour and are able to save four dollars (40%) on every ten dollars earned, in the long run you'll have saved more of your income than a person making twenty dollars an hour and saving four dollars (20%) per hour.)

The same analogy can be made with relationships. More importance is placed on how a person looks and what he or she says than what the person actually does in the relationship.

Believe me. I understand how important physical attraction is. Physical attraction is very important. It gets the car started, the ball rolling, the fire kindled. However, physical attraction is not the goal, solution, end and/or means.

Good looking people are sometimes more messed up than not so attractive people. Good looking people, as well as not so attractive people, have hang-ups too.

I'd rather have a girl that is secure with her unattractiveness than to have an insecure pretty woman that has to be told every five minutes how good she looks. I cannot carry anyone's self esteem for them.

Looks are temporary. One can find themselves with a disease or have an accident that leaves them disfigured for life. Where does that leave a relationship with physical attraction as its foundation?

A person's actions speak much louder than physical attraction. If someone really cares for you, the actions from that affection will follow suit.

He says, "I love you." But you can never find him. Actions speak louder than words. He says, "I'm a faithful man." But you keep finding girl's phone numbers on his person. Action speaks louder than words. He says, "I didn't mean to hurt you." But you found him in bed with another woman or *man*.

Action speaks louder than words and the proof is in the pudding. If it quacks like a duck—looks like a duck— trust me—it's a duck. It's exactly how you've seen it. You can't accidentally fall into bed with someone. Last time I checked, it's illegal to walk around in the nude. Your man made a conscious decision to get undressed and open the dessert pantry. He had plenty of time to stop. The Bible says, *"No temptation has taken you what is common to man; but God is faithful, who will not allow you to be tempted above what you are able, but with temptation also will make a way to escape, so that you may be able to bear it." **1 Co 10:13**.* That means, even if you find yourself in a compromising position, God will give you the opportunity to get out. Don't let him fabricate his way out of it. He wanted to do what he did. You're worth much more than being part of some man's harem. (Sorry, I got side tracked.)

Men have learned the art of conversation. He'll tell you anything "YOU" want to hear, so he can peel the panties.

Never ever believe what you hear at the first meeting of a man. He's got to come off a whole lot better than that. He's usually so blasted and drunk off of the testosterone surge, he's going to give you the best line of hog wash he can muster up in the brief encounter. And we're slick about it. We throw out a line (because we understand fishing) and see if we get any bites.

I was utterly surprised at some of the bait the women in my day took.

See, it takes very little effort to study a woman and find the keys to the dessert pantry. Most women are open books.

It takes a man of integrity to live a life of action. A man of integrity will be so busy with his plan of life, that he won't have much time to sit around and find ways to get into the dessert cabinet. He'll have straight talk for you if he's really interested.

A man of integrity will be mesmerized by your looks, but he'll contain himself—especially if he's ready to marry. Why? He's got just as much to loose by getting hurt as you do.

Give the man time to get over his intoxication. If he really likes you, he'll take the time needed to build a great relationship. Time pulls out the truth in all relationships.

Belief: I can get ½ of what I want in a man and fix up the other half.

Truth: After you fix the other half of him, he'll move on.

Women who repair men as a way of getting the relationship they want rarely benefit from their labor.

By becoming the handywoman in your relationship, you assume the role of his mother, grandmother or sister. No sane man marries his mother or sister, that's an incestuous relationship.

Always marry the man you can't live with out. Don't marry the man you can live with. That's a compromise or (in other words) that's settling for less than you deserve.

"He's crazy. It doesn't bother me." "He's a cheater. Oh, I can live with that—just as long as he comes back home." "He's lazy. Oh, I can change that." "He's physically abusive. Oh, I just need to stop upsetting him."

If you've got ½ of what you want in a man, I say, "It's better to keep it moving until you find the two halves in one man than to marry a half of man." Marry what you want. Strive for at least ninety percent of what you desire in a man. Don't spend the rest of your dating days and/or marriage trying to change your donkey into a thoroughbred race horse. Marry the race horse.

Always remember that men and women act their best while dating. If you marry half of what you want, after marriage the wanted half will be reduced to about a quarter of what you had while dating. That will not be enough of a man to keep the relationship together.

Belief: One day, he'll be true to me and to me only.

Truth: Once a cheater, always a cheater. If you let him get away with it once, he's going back to the dog that bit him (he's going to do it again). Every time you forgive him, your bite becomes less and less painful, and, the next thing you know, his cheating has become a way of life for you and possibly your family.

If you want a cheating man to stop cheating, a "relationship time out" will be inescapable. The man needs to know that your trust for him is just as important as the money in his bank account. The only way he'll learn to respect you sexually is for you to take some time away from him and let him earn his way back as the man of your life.

Of course you know if you call a relationship time out and he moves on, it's better for you. You don't deserve to be second, third or fourth. You deserve the best that God has to offer—a husband for you and you only.

Belief: I'm a good woman.

Truth: Sure you are. May I ask a question? Are you on the top of your game? Have you let weight loss or gain, or even laziness and complacent-ness creep in? Could you benefit from continuing education?

Even if you are at the top of your game, there's room for improvement. Read some books on relationships, self-help, finances, etc. Just because you have a job, a car, and a place to stay doesn't make you a good woman. A good woman knows her role in society. A good woman knows where she fits in God's will. A good woman understands how to be a good wife and mother. A good woman has allowed herself to heal from past hurts and tragedies.

Let's face this one fact. Most Black American families today are headed by women. Fathers are almost non-existent in our homes. I understand this plight very well, because I am a product of divorce. My mother and father's marriage went south when I was nine years old.

Because most fathers are almost non-existent, you will try to successfully marry someone you most likely don't know. I believe this is the greatest reason for 48% of Black American women never getting down to the alter. To make it as plain as possible, Black women don't get the day to day wife training they need from Dad being in the home.

However, just because Dad is not in the home, that is no excuse for not learning how to treat a man.

In order to be successful in anything you attempt, you must lend some learning time to it. In order to beat out your competition for a man without using your brownies, you must learn the art of being an enticing woman. You must learn to effectively communicate with men without your body parts' influence. You must learn to be the best you that you can be. Study to be a better you.

Belief: If I help him get his finances together or if I loan him the money, it's just temporary help.

Truth: If you help the wrong type of man (no destiny or purpose) once, you will continue to help him.

Why is it that way? Men are providers. God built us that way. Once you step in and become the so-called provider, you have taken the gumption or drive from the man to be the provider. The more you act like a man—the more you'll be treated like one.

I can say from experience. I've had some situations come up that were unimaginable. When I had my business, my family was in financial ruins. To briefly explain the problem, I had too much personal debt and not enough business income.

I remember when I was faced with the decision to return to work and I didn't want to. Reluctantly, I took the extra large "return to work" pill with some water and swallowed it with great difficulty.

I never asked my wife to go back to work. We were in so much financial trouble that when she asked me if she could return to work, I said, "Yes." Of course, I'm no fool. I agreed, because we desperately needed the money.

In the early days of "back to work," I barely had enough money to buy gas for commuting to and from work.

I remember hearing God's daily instruction on what to do financially. My money was just that tight.

You've got to really understand how horrific the situation was in my household at the time. The phone rang from 9 am until 9 pm. That's the legal time span that bill collectors are allowed to call.

Everyday, I had to make pertinent financial choices. During this time, I didn't ask any family members for money. The times were tough, but God ignited the provider inside of me and showed me how to navigate through the most intense financial time of our lives.

When you help a man financially, you get in the way of God / man connection and what really belongs to the man—self confidence and the learning experience. It's better to let the man fall into financial trouble and work his way out with God than for you to become the enabler. If you lend him money once, you've changed the way he thinks of you. Your color changes to pink. You become round and plump with a little curly tail and pointy ears. Does this sound familiar? It should. You've become his personal piggy bank and he will visit frequently for withdrawals.

Just as we are only to give minimal help to our children when they struggle with a task, so it is with men. Men need the fire turned up on them sometimes. In the long run it makes a better man of him.

When you loan him money, habitually, you not only get in the way of his God connection, you hurt yourself by becoming the financial solution.

Women were never meant to take care of men. How dare you get in God's way? How dare you interrupt a flow of authority set up by God Almighty?

Sometimes, love must be tough. Don't give in to the current crisis. Let him fall flat on his face. After the pain, a better man will rise from the ashes, and you will be ever so glad that you stood your ground.

Who changed the game?

As I mentioned earlier, high desire for sex on the man's behalf is to make a man seriously consider marriage. Before the *Sexual Revolution*, that's what the male sex drive accomplished for couples desiring to marry.

Before the *Sexual Revolution*, fornication was not glorified on, the big screen, television and in society. If you don't believe me, take a look at some of the older television shows like: *The Brady Bunch* & *I Love Lucy*.

Lucy and Ricky *(a married couple)* (from *I Love Lucy*) had two single beds in their bedroom.

The Brady Bunch (airing in the early seventies) was the first television show to allow a man and his wife to be seen in bed together. Back then, people were a little shocked by that.

Today, being in bed is not shocking, and some of the things done on television and in the movies have no shock value at all.

Back in the fifties, if you were in the bed with someone that wasn't your husband, your lips were kept tight on the matter. You may have possibly told your closest confidant, and you definitely wouldn't tell your classmates; because word would get around that you're easy.

Sleeping with someone back in the days of the fifties and early sixties contained a double edged sword. The guy you were messing with had to tell somebody that he hit it. And once the fellas knew that you were obtainable, they'd be all over you like flies on a steaming brown pile.

All a girl had was her reputation. Once she got a reputation for being easy, that rumor was not easily dismantled. Labeled girls were always remembered by their label for fifty plus years into the future. If you don't think that is true, ask your grandfather or father who was the easy girl back in high school.

Americans have gotten so far from the original plan of God that right is called wrong and wrong is called right. Meanwhile, while every one that claims to be right (abortion activist, same sex marriage advocates, etc.) has no advice for you when you make a decision based upon one of their lies. If you think that I'm too far on the right, after contracting a fatal sexually transmitted disease from living freely, go and ask an advocate of premarital sex for help with your medical bills. Ask them to heal you. Or better yet, after killing your unborn child, ask an abortion activist for financial help with your psycho therapy bills. See what they say when you tell them you can't sleep at night, because you hear your unborn child crying.

We fall for lies hook, line and sinker. In times past, I've been a victim of these lies. I was greatly influenced by my peers. My friends made me consider sex early on—before the onset of puberty. By the time puberty hit, I was desperate to get rid of my virginity. "I don't need this virginity baggage," was my primary thought about my sex life.

My friends pushed me to have sex, but the same friends never prepared me for what to do after the act was over. Many times because of guilt, I stayed with the girl in a "so-called" relationship long after it was over, because I could never be cruel to my soon to be ex. Being a soft hearted guy, I couldn't deal with the tears that most of my exes pumped out on cue.

Man, if she cried on me it only delayed the inevitable. I still felt the way I felt. The relationship was over. I just had to wait until the girl was stable enough for my disappearance.

Many of us, born after the *Sexual Revolution*, need to revisit the Bible to find out what the plan of God is for humans.

It is my belief that the rules in the Bible on fornication benefit women more than men—not to say that the rules in the Bible do not benefit men at all.

God wants all women to be protected and covered by marriage before having children. And because God ordained (created and authorized the family) two parents are required for the job of parenting. Two parent headed families (male & female) are the best possible situation for children. God never intended for women to be left holding the parental bag—which is so prominent today—especially among Black women.

Today, women are mothers and fathers—providers—homemakers—caretakers, etc. God never intended for women to carry this kind of weight.

Yeah, I know life isn't perfect. It's a learning experience. Many times, life will hand us some challenging situations that we've never dreamed of. If I could turn back the hands of time, I would do almost everything differently.

Many times, other people (like crazy spouses, boyfriends and girlfriends) make some stank decisions like—being unfaithful for one—that affect the course of our lives. If you're a casualty of this situation, make the best of it. However, don't get burned by the same fire twice. Don't feed the same dog that has bitten you in the past. The first time the dog bites you—shame on the dog. The second—third—fourth time the dog bites you, shame on you.

Life behooves you to find out "what's in it for me."
Life behooves you to separate facts from myths. The
Bible is the separator. Read it! It will show you the best
possible plan of attack for your life.

Don't accept the words of popular opinion as truth.
If it feels good, you can do it, but be ready for the
backlash.

Stock Market Rules

If female brownies were traded on the stock exchange, a mass exodus from the brownie stock would take place each day thus causing a rapid continuing decline of its worth or value.

What am I saying? In this country, we have a supply chain. The driving forces of the supply chain are "supply and demand." One drives the other.

If you have high supply and low demand, prices fall. If you have low supply and high demand, prices rise.

Remember back in the late nineties, gas prices were at an all time low? I remember finding a gallon of gas for $0.89 a gallon. Yeah, that's amazing.

In 2006, I've seen gas fetch its highest price in my lifetime. I paid $3.17 per gallon at an independent gas station in New Jersey. That wasn't the highest in the country, but it was definitely too high for me.

The cost to fill my car jumped from $22.00 to $43.00.

The steep increase made me reconsider where I drove my car. Walking became a good thing.

Why are we (Americans) willing to pay three and a half times the late nineties price? Gasoline and oil are key energy sources in the United States. We need gasoline to get to work, shop for food and clothing, etc.

In late summer of 2006 gas was high because of foul weather. That was the reasons the media gave us.

Hurricanes Katrina and Rita dismantled our already strained vital refining capacity in the Gulf Coast. So now the oil companies could demand more cash for the same product, because supply is low and demand remained the same. (It wouldn't be fare to blame the high prices all on the hurricanes. Greed has ruled the oil companies for the past three years.)

Also, OPEC (*The Organization of the Petroleum Exporting Countries*) continues to slow production of oil and its by-products. Why? Oil is a primary source of resources in many of those countries, when the oil is gone; it's likely that the lack of oil will impact the oil producing nations' way of life.

Since the late eighties, China's demand for oil has steadily increased. If the OPEC nations don't control how much oil is released for sale yearly, our demand and greed will deplete the reserves quickly. Then, the OPEC nations will be forced, in a relatively short period of time, to find another resource or source of revenue. That's why OPEC keeps closing the oil faucet. If they can command more money for the same resource, when their supplies are depleted, at least they'll have the financial resources to re-invest in their financial infrastructure.

The inversion is true also. High supply and low demand will drive the cost down.

In light of all the pressure from the oil companies, large SUV's have bore the brunt of the recent oil catastrophe. Imagine having purchased a vehicle that has a weekly fill up cost of about $50. Now imagine the fill up for the same vehicle skyrocketing to $100 or $115. Would you want to purchase that vehicle? Obviously, not—in fact, you'd probably try to cut your losses and dump the vehicle if you owned one.

The largest automaker in America got caught in the middle of the fuel pump war. GM was heavily invested in the large SUV market. When gasoline prices took its toll on America's pocket book, GM was left with a high inventory of an undesired product. What was their solution? Offer the country an employee discount. The plan worked. America bought the vehicles. However, the big employee sale cost GM a fortune, because the vehicles sold for 15% to 20% less than the MSRP (*Manufactures Suggested Retail Price*). A $50,000 vehicle was now retailing at $42,500.

The decrease in demand for SUV's did not work out in GM's favor.

What does this have to do with relationships? When you freely give your body to any man you feel like giving it to, it drives down the value of what you're giving.

The shear numbers of women willing to have premarital sex has driven down the value of sex and marriage.

Before the *Sexual Revolution,* a man honored his girl by marrying her and then having sex with her. Then after marriage, the children came.

In the past, there was a set order that the majority of Americans followed. Even when a couple messed up and a child was on the way, the man honored the woman by marrying her.

In the past, if you wanted to live with a man that wasn't your husband, you certainly couldn't do it in the town in which you grew up in, and you definitely couldn't do it in your parent's presence—let alone in the spare bedroom of your parents' home.

Now ladies, you're giving more and getting less. Yes. Supply is very high, and men (being the lesser in population) can't provide enough sex for the demand.

And, you ladies wonder why men act like fools when it comes to the brownies. You shouldn't wonder why some men act like fools. The men are just like children with the keys to the candy store.

Back in the fifties and sixties, men and women married. The life goals were as follows: get married—have children—and hopefully get rich.

Well today, as Black Americans, we are richer than ever before in American history—we have sex and children before marriage—and we get married less than ever before in our history.

Supply is so high that we (men) are at a daily sexual smorgasbord. With some men marriage is not considered a viable option, because they've lent themselves to the animal side of testosterone—too busy trying to sample all brownies near and far.

Ladies, you have to think like men think sometimes. We're not emotionally connected to you—even if we are having sex with you. Our connection takes time. We can separate fun from goals and objectives.

Ladies, most of you come unprepared for the game.

Every time you satisfy your man's sexual needs before marriage, you give the mule the carrot on the string before he's done any plowing in the fields. And then, at harvest time (when you're ready to be more than a jump-off), you wonder why there's nothing to eat in the winter months. (Why won't he marry me?)

If premarital sex was a commodity and traded on the NY Stock Exchange, it would be the least desired stock and would fetch a comparable price.

Demand for marriage is down because premarital sex is readily available. Like I said before, if the cow is giving free milk, what do we need to purchase the cow for? It's kind of difficult to make someone pay for something that was once free. It's not impossible, but difficult.

Cable television is a good example of taking a freebie and turning it into a cash cow. Of course, it took years for this concept to be accepted. And—not for nothing—

I'm beginning to reexamine why I'm paying for four hundred channels of nothing.

Ladies, you've got to become shrewd like the *OPEC* nations. You've got to get more for the same product. The only way to get more for your merchandise is to cut the supply. You'd be surprised to see how many "man games" will disappear once supply is cut.

Men have been on the premarital sex kick for over forty years. (That's not to say that premarital sex didn't exist before then. It did. But it wasn't as readily accepted by our culture as it is now.) It will take a while for the new rules and regulations to get imbedded in the minds of men.

We (men) have had a good run and it's been all at your (women) expense.

Some of you women sell yourself short. A man can take you to dinner a few times and to the movies. And the next thing you know, you're in some hotel room hollering and carrying on—having the time of your life.

Many women don't even get a simple dinner before breaking off the brownie. Yeah, the hotel hollering is fun for the moment. Toe curling fun is only a temporary entity—not the end or the goal.

Ladies, set your goals. Memorize your goals and keep them before you. If you want to be married, you must keep that as the point of focus internally. You can't mention your desires for marriage to the man on the first date—only after he has mentioned it in time, but you can certainly make sure that the guy you're dating knows up front that time is of the essence. You must always drive him to make decisions about you—the quicker the better. His decisions are always done via his thought process. You cannot make the decisions for him, but you must always make him make a decision about you. His thoughts and decisions will drive him to make one of these two decisions, "investigate more" or "I'm out of here." In either case you'll benefit from his decisiveness—only the serious need apply and hang around.

For example, if you say to a man, "I believe in waiting for marriage before having sex," he will think of his next move. If you were slated to be a jump-off, he's out. If not, he'll stay and get to know you.

Men can and will go back to the old school sexual habits. They just have to be steered in the right direction.

From the first time a boy has a "wet dream" he's thinking of ways to get into some girl's panties. He will do whatever it takes to make it happen. Ladies all too often underestimate the power of testosterone. Testosterone can and will drive a man towards marriage.

I remember when I was in the seventh grade. I walked past a table of my female peers at lunch time in the cafeteria. The pretty girls started to laugh as I walked by. I don't know if they were laughing at me, but I looked down and saw my stomach jiggling with every step I took. "It's time to go on a diet," I thought. And I lost the stomach in a few weeks.

Men want and desire women so much, that we are willing to do what ever it takes to make ourselves more attractive and acceptable to you. If we need to loose weight, we'll do it. If we need to make more money, we'll do it. If we need to get a fancier car, we'll do it. It's all because of the desire to be desirable.

Capitalize on the man's desire early. Just as the goals are in the stock market, keep the price of brownie high and on a steady incline. Someone will pay the price. And even if the stock is not affordable now, he'll work to be able to afford it. Yes, sometimes the price of a share of stock may be out of reach for some of us, but even when you find someone not willing to pay such a high price, someone else will come along willing to pay a good price for quality valued stock.

Ladies, I submit to you that this is the desired man. The man that is willing to go the extra mile to be in your company. Make us (men) do more for the same product. Trust me, you'll meet resistance at first, but when you (women) band together, the strong men will improve their game skills.

I remember a passage of scripture in the Bible (*Gen 29:16-20*). Jacob was on the run from his brother Esau and had gone down to see Laban his uncle. While there he fell in love with the beautiful and well-favored Rachel. Jacob told Laban, "I will serve you seven years for Rachel."

Laban agreed to Jacob's deal.

In verse twenty, it reads, *"And Jacob served seven years for Rachel, and they* (the days) *seemed to him a few days, for the love he had for her."* (Ladies, I submit to you that some of you can't wait seven minutes for a man that you love to marry you.) Jacob was willing to work seven years for Rachel. And if you keep reading the scripture, the total years Jacob waited for Rachel was fourteen, because Laban tricked him into marrying his oldest daughter Leah first.

But the Bible is very clear, Jacob loved Rachel. Jacob came to that conclusion all on his own without premarital sex clouding his judgment.

A good man will notice a good woman. A good man will put in the time to establish a relationship. A good man will care more about you as a whole person than what's between your legs.

A good woman is worth the wait. A good woman is worth working for. Are you a good woman?

Ladies, it's time for you to unionize. It's time for a united front against pre-marital sex. It's time to get more for less.

Don't let poor self esteem, poor judgment, competition and/or peer pressure rob you of what you really want and deserve. Have the highest value and expectations from life for yourself because you deserve the best that God Almighty has to offer.

No outside person will ever value a person that has internally devalued themselves.

Just as America needs gasoline, men need sex. Take a calculated risk in regards to your man's primary need—sex. You are worth far more than the average man is willing to invest.

A man of quality can respect quality and will pay the increase for quality stock. Cheaper and/or easier is not always the way.

Can and will a man contain himself sexually until marriage?

As a teenager, right after the onset of puberty, I was horny all the time. I remember praying to God that I wouldn't die before I got some brownie on a regular basis. Yeah, I know. That's kind of pitiful. But it's so true. It is my belief that this fear is real for any young man not engaging in sexual activities. Ask your brother or male cousin if this fear was prevalent in his teenage years.

At the age of fourteen, I lost my virginity. Then subsequently, I became a Christian, and because of Biblical reasons I didn't continue to engage in premarital sex during my teen years.

I wasn't a virgin when I came to know the Lord. So my prayer to God was, "Lord please let me get married before *You* return."

Even though my first sexual experience left a lot to be desired, I wanted to have more sex.

I knew that sex outside of marriage was Biblically wrong. So I desired to get married someday, because I needed to have some legal sex.

Lord knows I needed it. My body reminded me constantly of my need for sex. I'd be sitting in the classroom and find my mind had made my body react to some irrelevant sexual fantasy. Then the teacher would ask, "Irv, come to the board and help us solve this problem." I'd decline and take the zero, because I needed someone to help me with the problem banging on the inside of my zipper.

In my teen years, while I was a Christian, I had a couple of girlfriends. However, I never sampled the merchandise. I kept my gun in its holster.

Back in my youthful days, when I was overly horny, I'd feel a burning sensation in my chest. Yeah, the desire to have sex caused me to feel fire in my chest.

Even though most of the time I was unsuccessful with keeping my sexual thoughts in check during my years as a young Christian, I was able to keep my flesh in check. Thank God.

Now, I was able to do this in my teen years—the peak of hormonal overdrive for males.

Know this deep in your heart, "you can do whatever you want to do if you set your mind to do it. If you desire to refrain from sex until you marry, you can do it."

As a young Christian, I believed wholeheartedly in the Word of God and what the Word says about fornication. So therefore, I *decided* to keep my body in check. It wasn't easy. (But then again, anything *good* you do for yourself in this life will not be easy. The good things in life come with sacrifice.)

Life is full of challenges and decisions. I believe the most important debates in life must be put to rest by you and only you as soon as possible. You need to ask yourself some key questions as early as possible in life. Will you bend and follow the group? Or, will you be yourself and follow the principals that you believe in at all costs, even if it means parting with your best friend or that new and promising man?

Some other key questions to internalize are: "When will I start having sex? Who will it be with? And, how many sexual partners will I have?"

The earlier in life you make your decision (leader or follower), the better off your life will be. Always strive to live a life with the least amount of regrets. Make good decisions for yourself, because if the truth be told, most good men want a lady that can think and make good decisions for her self. We want a lady that's not so easily influenced by her family, friends and/or peers. We want a lady that is not so internally bankrupt that she makes bad choices with her body, money and soul.

I said all of that to say this, "a man can control himself if he wants to." If he's made up in his mind to wait on the right lady for marriage, he can and will do it. Ladies, believe that.

A man with spiritual convictions will be more apt to keep a lid on his libido than a morally bankrupt man.

If a man tells you, "I have to have sex no matter what," you really need to contemplate if that's the man for you.

A selfish man will be weak and take care of his libido—even if he is in love with you.

What if you are married and sex becomes too painful to endure because of a current female problem? Would you want to worry about your man running the streets because you're incapacitated briefly or indefinitely?

I'll give an example of temporary incapacitation. Right after childbirth, sex becomes a thing of the past for four to six weeks. The woman's body needs time to close and heal. Also, she needs time to re-establish her menstrual cycle. If you don't want another dead rabbit in the early weeks after the birth of your child, you must maintain some control. What if your so-called "man" can't hang on and be monogamous for the time it that takes your body to repair and begin menstruating again? I believe that that is a sorry excuse for a man, and you really need to re-evaluate your relationship if "no sex" temporarily will cause infidelity.

A decision to abstain from sex until marriage is equal to making a decision to remain in college until a degree has been obtained. "How bad do you want to get it done?"

If the truth be told, any man can abstain from sex until marriage. However, most men won't because of peer pressure, the sexual forwardness of women, ample brownie supply and lack of self discipline.

The ability for a man to control himself sexually will let you know what type of man you have. Leaders control themselves.

A lazy or un-disciplined man will be led astray by debauchery.

I must admit that I was un-disciplined for much of my twenties.

When I left the church, so did I leave my Christianity. The first sin on my demoralized agenda was fornication. And you'd better believe I got busy with accomplishing the task at hand.

When I walked away from my relationship with Jesus, I too, began to live by the world's philosophy, "if it feels good, do it."

Honestly, it did feel good for a while, but no one ever told me about the emotional pain that I would cause the women. No one ever told me about the emotional pain that I would be in.

A man connected to Christ is the best possible candidate for marriage. And if he is a true man of God, he will honor you and your body—before and after marriage.

A man hearing from Almighty God will cover you spiritually as he has been ordained to do, and although his body will yearn for you, he will keep his libido in check until the appointed time (honeymoon night).

The fear of my man leaving me for someone else with her legs open drives women to give her man access to her body that he hasn't yet earned. If you live by this fear, you will continue to make compromises with your body and get sub par results in your relationships with men.

A good man will wait for the appointed time for sex.

I suggest that when you meet a man, one of the first things you should tell him, "I believe in waiting until marriage before having sex." If he laughs at you, mocks you, or gets angry, you have just saved yourself much heartache and pain.

Look at the bright side of the laughter. He has just possibly saved you from being a baby mamma and all the drama. He has possibly saved you from a chronic or deadly STD. He has possibly saved you from being a part of a secret harem—which possibly includes his wife.

If he does not flinch when you state your sexual beliefs, it's highly possible that you've found a man ready to marry.

Men can and will control themselves sexually if put in the position. Men in their late twenties to early thirties actually want limits and boundaries. We're waiting on the woman that respects herself enough to put the sex brakes on. The woman that is brave enough to put the brakes on will see an increase in credibility from the man.

Never forget the fact that most men are opportunist. They'll wait if made to by the woman he cherishes. However if the brownie is presented, most times the opportunity will be seized.

The right man will wait for the right time to have you.

What are the methods of operation for men?

As a young pre-teenaged boy, I wanted to learn how to please a woman sexually, so I started reading women's magazines. I read them all—*Essence—Cosmopolitan*, etc. When I was a young teenager, I remember receiving two books in the mail—one book was about the man's body and the other the woman's body. Of course, I was more interested in the woman's book.

And of course, you guessed it; I didn't let my mother see me reading the woman's book.

The book was not meant to be pornographic. All of the pictures were drawn and it contained all of the proper terms. However, somehow the book of information was slightly pornographic for my inexperienced mind.

One thing the book described in detail was the stages leading up to orgasm. Now, that was just what I was looking for. I needed to be an expert.

The book explained what an orgasm would be like for the woman.

Too bad the book didn't explain how to con the panties off of women. I was an inexperienced expert in the orgasm department, because I didn't have the art of conversation. I needed an older brother to teach me. I was out of luck, because Mom certainly wasn't going to start looking for my Dad's possible illegitimate sons.

The point I'm trying to make is: study your opponent. I studied my opponent and eventually I became good at the art of telling women what they wanted to hear. Many times I was surprised with the results from my carefree blurted comments.

Women make it easy for a man to know the proper things to say. All we have to do is turn on *Lifetime,* pick up a girly magazine, join a women's support group or become the sympathetic ear at work for the girl in the next cubicle.

It's not quite that simple for women to read men— mainly because men are totally different then women. We don't think like you, internalize like you, feel like you, or even articulate like you.

We think about sex more than you. Yes, even your father and grandfather think about sex—even if the plumbing isn't working anymore.

Take a look at television aimed at male viewers. There's almost always a scantily clad woman somewhere in the mix.

Next time you see a big glass or bottle of beer, take note of the woman or women in the picture. Why are the women there? Men remember women. We can't help it.

I must admit one of my own faults. A colleague of mine made mention of a woman at work. She needed some information about our company. I had no clue of which woman he was talking about, until he made reference to a body part. (Sorry ladies.) At that instance, I knew exactly who he was talking about.

That's why women are in beer commercials. Advertisers know that men have a giant dump valve attached to their brains. We don't retain much. But, if you put a nice set of breasts next to what you're selling, there's a very good chance that it won't get dumped.

In order to get on the same playing field with a man, you must first understand a man's way of thinking.

Young girls learn how to interact with men by interacting with their dads. When Daddy is not there or the relationship between father and daughter is *strange,* girls usually try to deal with men from the woman's prospective—usually her mother's. (Fathers are supposed to be there to protect their daughters from the wiles of wayward men.)

This known fact is unfortunate for many young Black girls in our communities, husbands and fathers are like platinum—very rare.

At the beginning of a relationship, you cannot expect a man to deal with you emotionally, because he's not led by emotions. Emotional leadings are women's traits.

Most men are led by logic and reason. Men are hunters. We are built to provide.

Women are built for compassion. They are built to love.

For instance: A man and woman are driving in a truck together and see a deer next to the road grazing. The woman says, 'Awe, look at the beautiful deer grazing in the meadow.' As the man grabs his shot gun off of the rack behind the seat in the pick up truck he says, 'I bet we can eat for months on that.' These are two different responses from the same scene—one from emotion—the other from reason.

Another example: A man goes to the store with a shopping list. He's in and out of the store in a ½ hour. A woman goes to the same store with the same shopping list and she comes out four hours later with nothing in her hands. How is that possible? The woman was in the store touching and feeling everything that caught her eye.

The man, on the other hand, went only to the points of pick-up. The man accomplished the goal with the shortest routes taken.

So don't ever think that we're the same. Don't try to deal with a man from a woman's perspective. That's why there is a great communication gap in our society in regards to male and female relationships. Because of deprivation love, single women give sex to get the man, hold on to the man, mesmerize the man and hopefully convince the man that she is the one for him. (I pray that we will get more fathers involved in their daughter's lives. Teenage pregnancy would plummet.)

Single men have sex for gratification. Love has no room in the quest for gratification. Well, sometimes we get caught out there. But for the most part, we have separated emotions from objectives.

There are two types of single heterosexual men—the men that are ready to marry and the men that are not. No amount of sex will ever change a man's mind. Either he's ready to get married or he's not.

If your going to separate yourself from the pack, you've got to be able to get a man without your brownie being seventy-five percent of the equation.

A man must come to the decision to marry on his own through his own logic and reason.

You can play the emotional card if you'd like. You can play the "with child" card if you'd like. These methods and other forced methods only work temporarily, because the decision to marry belongs to the man.

Force a man's hand in any decision making processes and seeds of regret are planted in the man's heart.

Is Your Man Ready For Marriage?

Here's a brief list:

1. He buys himself something to eat, eats it in front of you, and doesn't ask if you want some. He has no problem with being inconsiderate.

2. He buys clothes with the rent money. Irresponsible is his middle name.

3. He asks to borrow a significant amount of money. There's no shame to his game when he borrows. He lacks integrity.

4. He treats his mother disrespectfully and/or dishonors his sister(s). Any man that dishonors the womb from which he came will have no problem with dishonoring you—womb man.

5. He's had more than three jobs in the past twelve months. It is highly possible that he lacks stability. This trait must be monitored closely, because driven men can have instability also. The key element to watch is; what is he doing in the background. He may be getting fired left and right, but if he's working on a secret recipe for BBQ sauce, that

might be worth hanging in there for. If he's not doing any other thing but talking about his dreams while constantly being ejected from jobs, it's highly possible that he is lacking in the responsibility area.

6. He's available only at his convenience, particularly during the booty call hours. It is what it is.

7. If he has children, he doesn't take care of them. Inwardly, he has something mentally wrong. A man that will not take care of the fruit of his loins is emotionally incomplete.

8. He's not forthcoming with his answers—too many inconsistencies and delayed responses. You'll never be able to trust a liar of commission or omission.

9. He never talks about future events that include you. Once again, it is what it is.

10. You've never met his mother, sisters, or aunts. Only real candidates for marriage get to meet the queens of his life. Believe me when I tell you, I wasted no time when it came down to bringing my future wife in front of my family. If the most important women in my life were not happy with my current choice, that would've caused me to take a few steps back and reexamine my choice. If you've never met the queens of his life, you're not being considered for a long term commitment.

First Things First

Men and women have universal needs. This discovery was expanded upon by Mr. Maslow. From his studies, Abraham Maslow created *Maslow's Hierarchy of Needs*.

The first of all needs are physical, and are shared by men and women. The need for clean air and water, food, clothing, sleep and shelter are all necessary to sustain life.

Jesus has been good to us here in America. He makes sure that the above items are available to us on a daily basis.

Although the US has its problems like all other countries, I thank God for the United States of America, because America is blessed.

After the basic physiological needs are met, safety concerns become the next priority or accomplishment.

Hungry and homeless people are not as concerned with the benefits of safety as with finding the next meal or somewhere to stay.

Safety concerns include finding a job or resources to support the primary physical needs.

Physical and health safety are also included in the quest for safety. The need for physical safety is the reason why society has designed laws and law enforcement.

The need for physical safety is also why many Black men are unfairly treated by our judicial system. The root cause of all judicial injustices is the fear of the loss of safety.

After finding a job that can meet a man's physiological needs as well as the physiological needs of others, the next need on the list is the need for friendship, sexual intimacy and family.

If a man is hungry and/or living on the streets, sex is not important. Even with his physiological needs going unmet, some men will take the opportunity for sex if it comes their way. But for the man who has his primary survival and safety needs met, you'd better believe he'll be on to the next thing on the pursuit list which is sex.

Ladies, when you give a Momma's boy premarital sex in his Momma's basement, you've skipped a couple of steps on *Maslow's Hierarchy of Needs.* Skipping steps, on the hierarchy, will only lead to trouble for you when and if you become his wife.

The next need for humans is: the need for love and to belong. Most men will never admit this to you while in the dating stage of life. This desire is real. We as men need love just as women need love. Although we have the ability to separate emotions from objectives, our need for love is slightly different from what you as women need, but we have the need just the same.

Many times, it takes a man a few years to realize that he has this need. Most good men (between the ages of 25 and 35) come to this realization: "I don't want to be a player all of my life." That is the need for love and to belong kicking in.

Now, there are exceptions to this rule. Some guys will realize this earlier in life (like in their early twenties), and some guys will want to be players until the casket. The player to the end always baffles me.

A good man will find his place of belonging in a family setting. In other words, there's something about being a husband and father that satisfies that love and belonging feeling.

On my wedding day, I felt like I had accomplished love. When my first child was born, I felt like I belonged. I know that it sounds corny, but that is how I felt.

God the Creator gave me a woman from His Creation allowed me to procreate and fulfilled my need to be loved and to belong.

Ladies, wait to find a man that has realized his need to be loved and to belong.

His desire to exit the "game" will be self evident by his settled mind and desire for a monogamous relationship.

SEX

Did you know that Adam and Eve were butt naked in the Garden of Eden and not ashamed? Did you know that before Adam sinned, God would visit with them and they were naked?

Oh yeah, God isn't far from you sexually. He is the designer of sex.

I am amazed at how the tricks of the devil have the entire world fooled. The devil wants you to believe, "God has nothing to do with that so-called nasty act." So if you believe that God has nothing to do with it, it's OK to do what you want. Why? We believe that God is not concerned with our sexual habits.

This could never be further from the truth.

God is the inventor of sex. Let me repeat it, so it can sink in. God is the inventor of sex. So, if God is the inventor of sex, we should be concerned with the rules and regulations He's set for sex.

For the record, heterosexual sex is only permitted in the context of marriage. Forgive me for being repetitive, but marriage in the Bible is defined as one man (born male) and female (born woman or man with a womb).

When two virgins marry, so long as they remain faithful to the spouse, sexually transmitted diseases are almost next to impossible to transmit to one another.

It is, however, possible to contract HIV via blood transfusion or by someone's bodily fluids (dentist, doctor, or bleeding friend).

So, you must ask yourself, why are sexually transmitted diseases running ramped if fornication (premarital sex) is not a problem?

Obviously, someone has a problem with premarital sex, if sexually transmitted diseases and unwanted pregnancies are the possible bullets that can strike you when playing the game.

No one has a problem with a sexually transmitted disease until it happens to them.

Sometimes you're lucky. If doctors catch gonorrhea or syphilis early, an antibiotic will take care of it.

But, God forbid if you get Herpes, chlamydia, or genital warts. You have to live with this baggage for life.

HIV and AIDS will definitely change the way you think about life and how much life you have left.

Premarital sex is serious; And God is just as serious about it.

Sex is a spiritual act. If not, the Bible wouldn't state... *Do you not know that your bodies are the members of Christ? Shall I then take the members of Christ and make them the members of a harlot? Let it not be!* **1 Col 6:15**

That means every time you decide to lay with a man, a part of you is taken with him and you are given a part of him—not just flesh and fluids—part of your soul (the inner you). If you lay with a pimp or a whoremonger, what does that make you?

In the Bible it says, *"A man should leave his mother and father and be joined to his wife and the two shall become one flesh."* This happens whether you're married or not, and it happens with anyone you decide to have sex with. Just think about that dude you met in the club and you didn't know his name, where he lived, or what he did for a living. He's running around here with a piece of your soul. Suppose he's a murderer? Or a child molester? Do you really want your spirit blended with his? And you wonder why every now and then you find yourself having relations with unknown men. You've picked up a piece of his wandering spirit.

The best place for sex is in heterosexual marriage.

I know you're probably thinking, "this guy is going to set women and men back five thousand years."

As a woman, you really need to consider what you're getting from this so-called "free love" era. If you look at the situation realistically, premarital sex is never free. And from the benefit standpoint, men are the true benefactors in sex without a marital relationship.

Today, a man can go to the bar, club, etc., find some unsuspecting girl, talk to her for a while, and take her on a few dates. After a few dates, she peels the panties. He gets what he wants and he's on to the next lady bus stop.

Two months later, she begins to feel sick, goes to the doctor, finds out she's pregnant and has chlamydia. She calls the guy to tell him about her new happenings. His reply, "look, you knew what you were getting into before you got into it. Get an abortion and some medication."

Now, you don't believe in taking a life. And even if you do support abortion, none of the abortion activist will tell you of the pain you'll feel for the rest of your life because you took life from your womb.

Now you have to drop out of college because the baby is coming. You take a job for 1/3 of the salary you could've earned if you'd finished college to support the child you never expected.

Who benefited from this situation? The man shirked his responsibility and moved on. Sure, he might feel guilty for a while. But as time goes on, his conscious will become seared. He'll forget all about you and the situation he created for you.

I wish you eighteen years of blessings; because you will need the blessings when it comes time to get your child support payments.

"That's an exaggeration!" I hear you screaming.

Not really. Of course, I made up the story. But I can guarantee someone can relate.

Ladies, please start looking at the situation realistically. Don't participate in the game, until you understand the game. Please understand that the game has been around longer than you.

From my point of view, the so-called "sexual revolution" has given you the short end of the stick in some areas regarding forward progress.

Since the inception of the revolution in the 1960's, women have lost some ground in the relationship area. Before the sixties, a man had to keep a lady's honor in tact before taking his sexual privileges. The stigma from society made it so. And if he messed up, there was an old term used in the south called "Shotgun Wedding." If the man messed up and knocked up his fiancé before the wedding, he had to marry her or be shot in the back by his girlfriend's father.

If the "Shotgun Wedding" approach was still in effect today, I believe that most men would put more thought processes into the "who will I be knocking boots with tonight?" Think about it. If he hit the wrong girl at the wrong time, he could very well wind up married to a girl he never intended to marry.

If the premarital sexual activity was cut off by young women, finding the right girl to settle down with would be more of a priority to men. Men would be more inclined to marry earlier and not waste women's fertile years playing the playa.

Remember, testosterone is at its peak from mid teens until the mid thirties—prime time for marriage and reproduction.

Women have taken away the incentive to progress to marriage. Men are enjoying all the privileges of being married without any real commitment. Whose fault is that?

If I went to the car dealer and the salesman just gave me the keys to a new car and let me drive it off the lot without asking for a check or a loan commitment, whose fault is that? Not mine. I'm taking advantage of the salesman, because the salesman allowed me. The salesman never stopped me and got the proper documentation up front. It is not my fault that he does not know how to conduct business.

After I've driven the car around for a week or two, I could possibly decide that that is not the vehicle for me. I'll take it back to the dealer or better yet, I'll sell it on *EBAY.*

So it is with women. Men are making all the decisions, and usually, you (women) get left holding the bag. And the proverbial bag usually contains diseases, an estranged or at home wife, children, heartache, deception—just to name a few.

I know it sounds bad. I'm talking of a life without sex until marriage. This sounds like it's from the Dark Ages.

Sex outside of marriage is fun. I know, because I've been there. But the amount of fun you have is equivalent to the amount of consequences you'll suffer for being prematurely sexually active.

I've had my heart broken, car stolen, gotten an ulcer and witnessed some nasty women fights. I was having the sexual time of my life, but on the inside, I was suffering.

I often think of a relationship I had in the past. I fell in love with this girl, but she was the wrong one.

She wasn't ready for the life I wanted. I knew three months into the relationship that I should've bailed. That would've been the perfect time for me to leave with no relationship cuts or scars, because we hadn't peeled any undergarments at the three month mark. But I continued, and eventually undergarments were peeled. I could've kept a clear head about the relationship in the beginning before we shared desserts, and I should've followed my first instinct "leave."

After the panties were peeled, I fell over her like a ton of bricks. I was "in love." Too bad she didn't know what love was. Too bad she was the wrong woman. After we broke up, it took me the better part of three years for me to seriously consider someone else for marriage. Wet blood was still leaking from my severed relationship cuts. I needed the wounds to heal.

To make a long story short, I wasted over thirty-six months of my life on someone that I was never going to marry. If I had only kept my flesh under control, I could've avoided years of tears and pain.

But I did the popular thing—I didn't resist the brownies. I could've saved myself a ton of cash in bar tabs and handkerchiefs. What a sad case I was.

Fear or Faith

Fear is the most destructive emotional force to mankind. I believe fear of failure has caused many of us to miss out on the greatest food recipes on the planet, miss the best inventions since the wheel, and miss out on the best opportunities for love.

Fear is very powerful. It is so powerful that the Bible speaks against it.

For God has not given us the spirit of fear, but of power and of love and of a sound mind. **2 Tim 1:7**

Usually, in the Bible, when you see the word "fear" it's used as a verb and is followed by the word "not." (Fear not.)

If you ever want to anger God, respond to His faith request with an answer from the center of fear.

Mankind gives fear too much power and control.

I believe that the rise in pre-marital sex is directly related to a core fear. (I don't want to be different from the crowd.)

Fear is not the only reason for pre-marital sex. But from a woman's point of view, unrealized fear has directly contributed in the decision to give up her virginity long before the appointed time.

Simply put, the world (some Christians and most non-Christians alike) simply does not want to have faith in God in the relationship department. The world does not want to rely on Him to pick and send a compatible heterosexual spouse.

We are always drawn to what we want. It's hard to trust God, because He'll give you what you need.

Fear also keeps a lot of unqualified men in relationships that they are not worthy of. Women fear getting old with out ever meeting the right man. Women fear living alone. Women fear other women will take their man. Women fear not being able to give a man a son. Women fear a better man will not come. Women fear that they can't live without a man. Women fear that they cannot succeed without a man. Women fear that they'll never bear children.

I've been a victim of my own fears. It's not a good place to be, because fear will rob you of what really belongs to you in this life.

This life, as it is here on earth, is not a practice run. We don't get to do it over. All the time wasted is gone forever. All the time wasted in fear is lost—never to be regained.

Think of all the sub par things you tolerate in your life. You hate your job. You don't like where you live. You're dissatisfied with your finances. You want that crusty dude called your "man" to get out of your home.

"I want that man to get out," she thinks, but never takes action.

Why no action? After she digs deep in her soul way past the procrastination, she'll find fear somewhere down in there as the root of the problem.

"If I throw him out, can I really pay all the bills by myself?"

Realistically, if the woman would take a good look at her situation, she probably wants him out because he can't keep a job, and she's already paying her bills plus carrying him from month to month. She can throw Crusty out if she ditches the fear.

Every woman deserves a good man, and fear should never ever be the driving force behind the decision when choosing a man.

Fear will always cause you to live beneath your means. In other words, fear will cause you to become dependant—accepting less than you deserve, compliant—staying in the rat race (common path) of life with no room for your dreams, and complacent—never changing the set of circumstances in which you were born.

In life, there are two methods of operation in the area of success: fear—passive and faith—proactive.

Passive fear will cause you to rationalize with what's in plain view of you and internalize, "this is not so bad, I can live like this. I can make it."

Proactive faith says, "even though I can't see the better thing I desire for myself now, I know something better will come if I sacrifice what I have and go for it."

Faith is always a stretch. One will never physically see what they're reaching for in faith until some time, work, and diligence takes place.

"If I tell my new beau that he's not having sex with me until he marries me, I'll never get a second date."

"If I tell my new beau that he must have a job and a place to live before I'll go out with him, he'll find someone else."

"If I don't give him some brownie, he'll get it elsewhere."

The fears listed above are real but not justified. The only way the fears have power is if the woman with the thoughts make decisions and/or take actions based upon the fear thoughts.

Not all men require sex to be in a relationship with you. A good man's sexual accomplishments will not be tied to his manhood.

Yes, if you don't give some men sex, they will most likely find it elsewhere. But that shouldn't matter to you. Why not? If he can't contain himself long enough to marry you, it's highly unlikely that he'll be sexually faithful to you if you should marry him. Is that what you want—a sexually unfaithful man? Most women don't want their boyfriends to cheat on them. But because of fear (I'll have to find another man. No one better will come along), women will ignore the sixth sense (woman's intuition) and look in the other direction when their man has periods of time that he really cannot give an account.

No one has ever succeeded in life with "fear" as the captain. So, with that said, I believe the underlying motivation in dating and spouse seeking must be searched. If fear is at the root, all decisions will be based upon today's circumstances and not tomorrow's truths.

You'll need gumption to move by faith. Fear will give an easy excuse to explain away the lack of accomplishment.

Every decision you make concerning life must be searched. Is it from God or from a secular view? Remember, God didn't give us the spirit of fear, so why should fear have "decision making power" in anything we do?

Fear entered the world as a result of sin from Adam and Eve. At the risk of repeating myself, God didn't give us the spirit of fear; therefore fear is unnecessary for success in life.

If you want to be married to a good man, don't settle for less. Don't let fear drive your relationship decisions.

Each and every time you meet a possible candidate for marriage, fear will always appear. A fearful woman will cause a woman to have the *Band-Aid* approach with the new beau. (I can fix him.) A fearful woman will rationalize away all questionable behavior from her new or old beau. A fearful woman will sacrifice and trash her virtue all in the name of keeping her beau. A fearful woman will stay in a relationship with her beau long after it's over in fear of not meeting anyone else equal to the *trash* that they need to dump. A fearful woman will sacrifice her public dignity for a no good cheating man. A fearful woman will allow a man to physically beat all life and hope from her.

Be encouraged! Be encouraged! On the opposite side of fear is *faith.* Grab on to faith and never let go of it.

Faith looks at impossible situations (relationships) and says, "It can be done."

Faith is full of power—power to change. Faith is full of love, and sometimes tough love says, "No." Faith is full of sound decisions. Faith will make the hard decisions—even if it means taking a loss.

Fear only has as much power as you *give* it.

Why get married?

If you are selected for marriage (the key word is: selected), God's best for you is to be under His covering until you and your husband hook up. After that, you are under your husband's covering. Your husband is the leader and protector of the home. He's the one responsible for what does or does not go on in the home.

And rest assure in this fact, your husband or baby's daddy will stand in judgment by God and give and account of what he did or did not do on behalf of his offspring.

One of the major challenges we have today in the Black family is women are the heads of households. Many of our (Black) families are living by the shotgun blast's end result. The blast from the pellets is deadly and the kickback from firing the weapon is almost as painful as your flesh being filled with pellets.

What does the previous statement mean?

Women are on the receiving end of the shotgun pellets. They're forced to raise some shiftless man's children alone.

The shotgun kickback hurts the children too. By women heading Black families, many generations of girls and boys are finding themselves a secondary casualty. Growing up fatherless is the life they will face.

I believe the shotgun kickback is worst than the initial blast. Mothers cannot effectively raise boys to be men. Some women have more success than others (like my mother), but growing up fatherless is not the best that God has for us. I know, because I lived it.

Boys need real men to teach them to be men.

As I've said a few times before, the Bible says, *"For this cause a man shall leave his mother and father and be joined to his wife."* That's God's best for relationships—marriage—husband and wife—then possibly children.

I wonder what is happening. So many of us Black people are breaking through the church doors on Sunday morning. However, somehow we are living far from God's best.

The children are suffering the most from the lack of marriage in Black America.

If a single mother has not established respect from her son in the early years (4 to 10), she'll never gain it during the puberty years.

Raising a son or sons is very different than raising a daughter or daughters.

Testosterone has a few vital components—one of them is fearlessness. Higher levels of testosterone, makes a man more likely to take risks (racing, mountain climbing, gambling, risky financial investing, building skyscrapers to give a few examples). The surge in testosterone early in life is highly necessary. Young men need to take higher risks earlier in life. That way they can recover should a setback take place.

A young man will take a job cleaning windows on a skyscraper. But most times when that same man gets around thirty-five to forty years of age and his level of testosterone drops, it is highly probable that he'll look to change his career to something safer. And if he doesn't, he'll begin to express his unhappiness with the daily risk factor that never bothered him in the past.

When fearlessness enters the game, boys that have a respect-less relationship with their mothers, tend to be hard headed and unleashed. Some boys will even strike their mother if she tries to get in the way of their wrong doings.

This is where Daddy comes in. Daddy will let the boy know, "under no uncertain terms will you touch his wife. If you do, I will kill you." (Not literally, but he'll wish he was dead.)

Whenever any of my children get out of line when speaking to my wife, I sternly ask them, "Who are you talking to? I know you're not talking to my wife like that."

I say it like that for two reasons. The first reason is: I want my children to understand the pecking order. My wife was my wife long before any of them were born. She was my wife long before she became their mother. The second reason is: My wife belongs to me. She's not a piece of property; however she is someone that I care about deeply. I want my children to know that when they mouth off to her they are disrespecting someone that I care for, and it will not be tolerated. (Sidebar: I don't want her coming to bed all stressed out from my children. How can I benefit from her being stressed out at bedtime?)

Furthermore, my son is always watching what I do. When I tell him to stop talking, or sometimes when I pop him in his trap for mouthing off to my wife, I'm teaching him to respect my wife and women in general.

Women are not in the position of authority to demand that kind of respect from pre-teen and teen boys, unless they're willing to inflict some serious bodily harm on the boy. That's what my mother did. (Well it wasn't that bad. I'm living to talk about it.)

Usually, the guy that had no respect for his mother's authority over his life finds himself in a fix like incarceration, because hard-headedness ruled the way.

See, daddy is a man. He understands exactly what the boy is going through, what he is thinking and how he processes daily challenges, because he's been there.

Mom can only teach her son how to treat a woman from a woman's perspective.

While women are raising our sons, our sons become more prone or adapted to responding to his feminine side—thus perpetuating the problem.

No doubt during his childhood, the fatherless son learned the buttons to push to get Mommy to respond in the way he wanted. Most fatherless men know how to sweet talk women into the bedroom, but the same men don't know what to do after that. That explains why Black America has the highest rate of single parent homes. Our fathers need to return home, and teach our boys to be men.

So, when you hear your boyfriend speaking that foolishness in your ear about having his baby, think about your contributions to our race. Are you part of the problem, or part of the solution?

On the flip side of the coin, girls need to see men leading in the home. If a girl grows up in a home with Mommy as the primary parent, this adds to our plight.

At one time in my life, I wondered where all the hostility towards Brothers from Black women came from.

I believe the hostility starts long before any man does them wrong. This hostility is passed on from her mother.

Mom is a single parent. Why? Mom's man burnt her and left her holding the bag. When many Black women get together for chit-chat, the common theme is: "I don't need no man." Excuse the English. But that's how it goes down.

Our daughters have the pleasure of witnessing you, her mother, calling her current boyfriend or ex-husband everything but a child of God behind his back—hearing you cuss out the man at the gas company because they turned off the gas for non-payment—fight with her daddy for child support.

(Most of what you are saying about her daddy may be true, but please keep it to yourself.)

After hearing all this negative press (truth and lies) the girl must come up with her own method of operation so that what happened to Mommy will never happen to her. And that is where the slogan: "I don't need no man" comes in.

Fatherless homes hurt all involved. Girls need a male figure around to keep the hounds at bay. Girls also need a male figure around to learn how to communicate and act around a man.

The man's nonexistence in the Black family home has caused a communication gap from women to men. Unlike the young girls, the fatherless men are learning to communicate with women throughout their young lives—and they get quite good at it.

A man will never start a conversation with an intended prospect like this: "let's have hot passionate sex a few times until I'm tired of you. Then, after I find out you're pregnant with my child, I'll ditch you for the next woman with less baggage that catches my eye. And, every now and then, I'll stop by to tap it just so you can remember what you could've had." We never say that, but that situation is reoccurring every day. The fatherless men have learned to say one thing and do another.

The fatherless women become victims of the wiles of men. Where are the fathers that are supposed to protect them?

I have two daughters. One of my daughters is eleven years old. Sex or even the thought of sex is still something to giggle about. She thinks sex is funny. She's already learned about the anatomy of the female and male body.

We talk about sex now, because I want her to be very comfortable talking to me about sex. (Trust me. I've got my own internal concerns to deal with. It's frightening to think that my baby girl will one day look like a woman.) I want to be the first person considered when she has a question to ask about what some boy has told her.

Sometimes we get into discussions about clothing. She sees all these young girls with their stomachs and booty cracks hanging out, and she wants to dress that way.

I tell her, "If you ever want a man to respect you, you must first respect yourself." (If you dress like a sex object, don't be surprised when he treats you like a sexual play thing.)

I want to be the chief sounding board for my daughter. I will dispel all of the myths the young players try to run on unsuspecting girls.

Also, when she starts dating (long after high school) (I see no need in my daughters or son for that matter, dating while in high school. They are not ready to marry and it is a recipe for disaster. If you're not old enough to marry, what is the purpose for dating while in high school?), I want to see who she is going out with. I want to know where he lives. I want to know who his parents are. Most of all, I want to know, "WHEN ARE YOU BRINGING MY DAUGHTER BACK?" And if you don't have her in here when you said you will, you'd better have car troubles or something, because that will be the last time you'll see her.

You can laugh if you want. But, parents need to become parents again. This is the primary reason why teenage pregnancy is as high as it is. Young boys have no one to be held accountable to. Before the sixties, every boy had to come and meet the girl's father. Usually, Daddy would find this to be an excellent time to clean his shotguns and pistols—just so he'll get the message.

I heard a father on a Christian radio station many years ago. The man's daughter was of dating age. Well the young man stopped by to pick the girl up for the date. The father noticed that the boy had taken an old beat up car and turned it into a gem.

The boy's date was a little delayed in greeting him at the door. So the father welcomed the boy inside and they talked briefly while the boy waited for the girl to come down the stairs.

Just before leaving, the father pulled the young man aside and said, "You've got a nice car. How long did it take you to get it into tip top shape?"

"It took me about twenty four months," the boy replied.

"It sure must have cost a lot of money," the father replied.

"You bet it did. I had to work after school and summers to get the money for the repairs," he replied.

"I noticed that there are no dents or scratches on the car," the father continued.

"No sir. I take very good care of my car," the boy replied with a smile. "I wash it once a week—change the oil regularly—and make sure it's mechanically sound."

"See that you care for my daughter in the same manor in which you care for your car. I've invested much more time raising my daughter. Don't bring her back all scratched and dented," the father said with a serious smirk.

At that moment, the boy pushed down his smile of pride and said, "I will."

Boys need to know, "if you can't control your urges and mess up my daughter, you'll have to see me (Daddy) about the damages.

There's no fear of Dad, because dad is not in his rightful position.

If you ever want to ask the question, *"why get married?"* The answer is, "it is God's best for my children and me."

Young girls need to see men as authority figures. They need to have the privilege of watching a man rule his home well. Young Black girls need to have the privilege of seeing their mothers happy and in love with a good man (preferably their father). Young Black girls deserve the privilege of protection from their dad's loving arms.

Young Black boys deserve the right to be taught to be a man by their father. Young Black men need to learn that it is never OK to take advantage of young Black women. Young Black men need to have the loving arms of their father open to them.

Men and boys need love from other men and boys. I hate to say it, but I believe that the rise in homosexuality among young Black men is directly related to the need of affection from the non-existent Dad.

You know when my son was a little tike; I'd grab him by the head and kiss him on the back of the neck.

After months or possibly years, one day out of the blue, my son grabbed my giant head and pulled it down to where he could reach me. He kissed me on the back of my neck. It was at that moment that I realized that my son needed those kisses on the back of the neck just as much as I needed to give him those kisses on the back of his neck.

To this day, he'll walk up to me and give me a kiss on the cheek and a great big bear hug. And you know that I still kiss him on the neck. I still give him a hug.

Recently, my preteen son was given a homosexual proposition by another boy his age. He stopped playing with the boy. Weeks later, my wife and I asked him, "What happened to so and so?" My son told us about the proposition and said that he turned him down. He also said that he didn't think that he and the other boy could be friends anymore.

Well, my son and the boy became friends again, because my son straightened the boy out (not physically).

To this day, I often wonder what kind of choice my son would have made if I never kissed him on the back of his neck.

My son would be like the millions of fatherless sons searching for daddy's love in all the wrong places.

That's why we as Black Americans should seriously consider marriage. Let's give our children and generations beyond our life span an opportunity to have the best that God has to offer—and as my Momma used to say, "Charity (or love) begins at home."

Let's start building great homes again.

Children

The Bible says, *"Lo, children are the inheritance of the Lord: the fruit of the womb is a reward."* **Psalms 127:3**.

When I grew up in a single parent home, we were the poorest family in my neighborhood. Food was most times scarce. Money was almost non-existent. And I saw my daddy only a handful of times from the age of nine to twenty.

My mother was always on an emotional roller coaster, because she was the mother and father of five children. As I lived life with mother, I witnessed her life's struggle first hand.

During my teen years and early twenties, I've seen many teen girls and young women pop up with the big belly. (Thank God it wasn't happening to me. I mean. Thank God none of the girls were having my baby.)

Because of the number of girls my age with children, I've dated a many a single mother. I've even dated a divorced mother with four—that's right four children.

I married at the age of twenty-seven. My first child was born in my twenty-ninth year. And now, as I write this, I have a total of three children. Thank God for my children. I love them dearly.

My wife and I are the primary caretakers of our children.

At times, our children need to be in two different places at the same time. Or one needs help with homework, while the other has gotten in trouble in school.

Child rearing is a daunting task—even for married couples.

I said all of that to say this. I love my children, and I never want to think of my life without them. However, if I were to trade places with women—knowing what I know now—there is no way on God's green earth that I would have a child or children outside of a heterosexual marriage. You couldn't pay me enough money to open my legs and have your child and you (the man) have no commitment or obligation to me.

When I dated the divorced woman of four children, her oldest son was six years younger than me. (How could I be his daddy?) I was twenty-two years of age and she was eleven years older than me. She was ready to start a new life. At twenty-two, I hadn't even started my life.

She began to talk of marriage. I wasn't ready to give her more than what we already had.

During one of the many conversations about our future together, she told me if we married, I could possibly have one child. (What a deal.) Child birth for her was a chance in itself, because two years before we met, she had an operation to untie her fallopian tubes.

This lady was a good woman. I'd come over the house and be treated like a king. She cooked very well, and knew how to treat a man.

In the end, I had to leave, because it wasn't a good deal for me. Why? Honestly, she was too old. I was just starting my life and she was starting over. But I must say the weighted reason for not marrying her was the amount of children she had. I was not about to marry (or should I say re-marry) into my mother's plight. I was trying to get away from it.

There is a time and season for everything. Believe it or not, the season for having children is after marriage. When you make premature decisions in the wrong seasons of life, consequences are coming.

Ladies, stop having babies by men who won't marry you.

When men are looking to marry, we don't want a woman that has been around the track so many times that her feet are full of bunions, corns and calluses. We don't want a ready made family either. We (young men) want the opportunity to make or produce our family from our own loins. That is a desire given to us by God.

Also, we want to have as many children as "we" desire. The minute you (women) allow another man to impregnate you, your position as a viable candidate for marriage has dipped. For instance; if you had a hundred percent chance of marrying man A, once he finds out you have a child, your chances may dip to ninety percent. You've become less desirable as a possible candidate for marriage because of a previous decision or mistake.

Another example: A man meets a woman. They talk. He finds out she has three kids by three different daddies and she's twenty-six years of age. If he was ready to get married, the game plan shifts. He won't tell her—even if he was looking for a wife. Now, he'll just try to get into her pants because he knows that is a good possibility.

Why would a single man with no children want to get involved with all of the baby's daddy drama?

At the risk of taking heat over the subject of premarital children, women must make better choices in regards to birthing our next generation—our children. We all make mistakes in life. Babies out of wedlock have been born since the Bible days. God can bless us and our children planned and unplanned—even if it was one of our greatest mistakes.

But, why submit to a way of life that will be tougher than anyone can imagine? Why submit to a life of insurmountable challenges?

Five minutes of pleasure can cost you twenty-one years of struggle.

Children are not all bad. Ask any unwed mother, and she'll tell you, "There's nothing in this world that compares to being a mother. I wouldn't trade my motherhood for anything in this world."

Deep inside that same mother's heart whispers, "Don't get me wrong. I love my children but, if I could do it over again, I should've waited for the right man to come along."

I know your thinking, "but what about the men that have baby's mamma drama." If I were a woman and met a man with five children by four different mothers, I wouldn't consider him for marriage either. Why would I want to live a life with a man that has sixty percent of his check going to the mothers of his illegitimates? How can we accomplish anything financially? How many children will he desire after already fathering a baseball team? It's quite obvious to all of us. He'll be limited in regards to his family size and financial accomplishments, unless he's got large—very large paper.

The Bible is true. Children are an inheritance from the Lord, and the fruit of the womb is very rewarding. Our children are supposed to do better than we have done— or accomplish more than we've accomplished. That is our (the parents) portion or inheritance or legacy.

But we've put the horse before the cart. Children are supposed to come after marriage. If divorce should happen after the children, that is most times an unfortunate event and is another three or four hundred page book.

The way God designed the system is for men and women to meet, marry and then have children. If we don't follow the order set up by God, then we set ourselves up for the consequences that will soon follow—financial and social single parent struggles—less desirability as a likely candidate for marriage—wayward children because of imbalanced families (no fathers present).

The best possible advantage in life that you can give your children is to be born into a family with a father and mother present and paying attention.

When I dated back in the mid eighties and early nineties, I had no children. Yeah, I know that's hard to believe. For a while my girlfriend (now my wife) thought I had a couple of kids across town.

My sister verified my claims of being childless.

However, when I dated, I was willing to give a single mother of one child a chance. I figured—one bad decision shouldn't be punished for a lifetime.

If a female had two or more children, I would not consider her as a formidable candidate for marriage. Why not? One baby out of wedlock is a mistake—two babies and above is no longer a mistake, it's a way of life.

A woman that has two or three babies or more without a husband is not a goal oriented person. A woman that has more than two unwed babies is letting the circumstances of life run it. That's not my type of woman. Most good men won't desire this type of woman either.

The best thing that anyone can do for his or her self is learn his or her purpose in this life on earth. The sooner you learn your purpose, the less chances you have of getting off track or going somewhere in life that God never intended for you.

Having children out of wedlock by two or four different people is "NOT" God's will for anyone. The only way I can see it legitimately happening is if a person has three children by three different deceased spouses.

It's not in His divine purpose for you to spend the rest of your days fighting over child support. It's not in his will for your children to be neglected by the mothers and fathers of the illegitimate children. It's not the will of God for children to be born to unwed parents.

When the decision is made to have sex with someone that's not your spouse, please note that the chances for an unwanted pregnancy are highly possible.

After having the baby, your chances for marriage has been diminished significantly.

What does that mean? If ten candidates for marriage suddenly appeared, upon finding out that you have children from previous relationships, your chances for a relationship with two to four of the ten men or women has been eliminated or significantly reduced.

And here is the good part. You will never know that you've been disregarded as a viable candidate, because it's highly unlikely that he'll openly confess his intentions.

Hurt and Pain

Ladies, if I could put my finger on the one set of emotions that can kill your hopes and dreams in a new relationship, those emotions are "hurt and pain" from previous relationship(s).

Hurt and pain are the greatest stumbling blocks for a new relationship. The new person is treated unfairly. He or she has to overcome all of the damaging things that the old person did.

The unfair advantage causes many of "would be" spouses to keep it moving. After all, why should he or she stay in a relationship where the odds are against them? Why would he or she stay in a relationship of constant proving and reassuring?

People of the past are people of the past for the obvious reason. It didn't work out. If it didn't work out, both parties involved in the relationship are at fault. Yes, I said it.

He cheated on me. Perhaps, you didn't wait long enough to find out that he was a womanizer.

He stole my money. Perhaps, you gave him way too much information too fast.

He got me pregnant and left me. Perhaps, you ignored his selfish and irresponsible ways.

These are only a few basic things that a man can do that will cause hurt and pain.

In my lifetime, I've seen and heard of men doing dastardly things—like sleeping with their girlfriend's mother or sister.

Life is funny, because sometimes the best thing that could ever happen to you can come right after one of life's most insane incidents. If you're not careful, the past storm of life will rob you of your destiny.

I've found a good way to deal with hurt and pain. "GET OVER IT!" There is no secret formula. The only formula that works is to forgive all those involved, forget about the incident and keep on moving forward.

Nothing is ever solved in life by hanging on to hurt and pain. In fact, life will stop in its tracks. Even if something new and exciting comes your way, you will not recognize it because of the hurt and pain.

I've observed people and myself in regards to hurt and pain. People, filled with hurt and pain, are very stereotypical. He or she believes that everyone is the same and there is no use in giving anyone new a chance.

People, filled with hurt and pain, are operating under the same spirit as racist. Racist people always make general statements about people that are of another race. The racist never takes the time to get to know the individual for who he or she is. That is so unfair.

Nothing can be more frustrating to the new man or woman than competing to change how he or she is perceived by the significant other. Most people cannot handle that kind of pressure, so they run for the hills.

Forgiveness for being wronged is where it all begins. It is the pathway to recovery. Forgiveness is the first step in moving forward.

You know what I found out? Hanging on to hurt and pain only hurts the person holding on to it. The one who caused all of the hurt and pain has moved on and will deal with his or her devils later. And believe me; no one is free from the consequences of life. You may never see it happening to them, but just because you haven't witnessed their payback with your own eyes, doesn't mean that it hasn't or will not come.

Forgiveness is for you not for the individual that wronged you.

Forgiveness releases you and allows you to move forward.

The next step is to forget about it. When the thoughts come to your mind, think of something else. Think of your goals, aspirations and the good things of life. Don't rehearse the hurt and pain. Don't sit around thinking, "woe is me." Cancel all future pity parties. You are not the first person done wrong by a man or woman—and you won't be the last. FORGET ABOUT IT! It is easier said than done, but you must forget. Your future depends on it.

My mother, God rest her soul, never forgot what my father did to her. I know in my heart that my Dad was sorry for what he did. We all make mistakes. But that didn't matter to my Mom. She never forgot, and she never found happiness with someone else. She died a divorcee.

My mother and father's marriage was over in 1975. My mother lived to May of 1994. Although, she had a few male friends through the years, I believe she never remarried because she never forgot what happened to her nineteen years earlier.

Some women have suffered longer than that.

All men are not alike. There are some good men out there. Good men are challenging to find just as it is challenging to find good customers, a nice neighborhood, and/or an excellent job. Although it's challenging, it can be done. And it's worth it.

Besides, if good men fell out of the trees, you ladies would go crazy—treating men with disregard. You see, sometimes you've got to drink vinegar so then and only then will you appreciate being served grape juice.

(I've dated many Broom Hildas before I dated my wife. And believe you me, when I found myself in a relationship with my wife, I was respectful of that relationship, because it was challenging to get there.)

The final move in regards to "hurt and pain" is moving forward or opening yourself up to allow space for someone new. That means canceling the spirit of relationship fear. You've got to learn from your past mistake. You've got to be confident that you've learned from the past mistake. You've got to be confident that you will not under any circumstances repeat the last mistake(s). Once the confidence arises, there is no stopping you. You are ready to give the next person the full opportunity to be your spouse.

I hate to keep repeating myself, but most of the hurt and pain we find ourselves in is all because of the body parts between our legs. If we could just put sex aside and in its proper context we would avoid so much of life's agony.

In this day and time, no one wants to be horny. Being horny is not a good thing, but the alternatives to not being horny can possibly kill you.

How much drama in your life comes from your genitalia?

It's all mental!

I read the Bible a lot. I know almost everyone out there has seen *Cecil B. DeMille's, "The Ten Commandments."* It's the story of God, thru Moses, leading the children of Israel out of Egypt's bondage.

I love that movie. I've been watching it since I was a kid.

I remember the scene when Moses' brother Aaron laid down his staff and it turned into a snake. Then, Moses' snake devoured the other two snakes Pharaoh's magicians created from their staffs.

I remember the scene when Moses spread his arms out to open the sea.

I also remember the scene when Moses came down from the mountain and slammed the commandment tablets into the ground right next to the worshiped golden calf.

I love that movie.

However, the movie doesn't cover the entire story of the Israelites' journey to the promise land.

In the thirteenth chapter of Numbers, the Israelites had reached their destination, and the Lord told Moses to send out twelve spies to search out the land of Canaan. Twelve went out and ten came back crying and complaining about how big the people were that occupied the land. Less than twenty percent (16.67%) of the spies had enough faith to believe that the giants that occupied Canaan could be evicted.

Then the Israelites began to complain, *"...If we had only died in Egypt! Or in this desert! Why is the Lord bringing us to this land only to let us fall by the sword?"...*
Numbers 14: 2-3

I often wonder how I would respond to the Lord if he told me I had a land flowing with milk and honey, but there's one catch. You'll have to take it from an army full of seven foot tall men. That may not seem like much of a challenge if the average size the men in my army were six foot five.

But if we averaged at the height of five foot five, I might have questioned the Lord. "Are you sure that this is what you want us to do?" Chuck Norris, Steven Segal or Billy Blanks hadn't been born yet. Who would teach us karate?

The ten spies' negative report had more of an impact on the Israelites than the good report from the two spies. The murmuring and complaining from the Israelites was so bad that it angered God. And God Almighty was ready to clean house. But Moses pleaded with God and saved the hides of the Israelites.

However, as a punishment for disbelief, the Israelites that did not believe and complained were doomed to death in the desert. (**Numbers: 14:22-24**)

The two spies that faithfully believed the land could be taken; the Lord promised them life to out live the death sentence of the other non-believers. And when it was all said and done—forty years later—the two spies along with the children of the disbelievers occupied the promise land.

(I encourage you to read the account of the Israelites' journey out of bondage and into the promise land.

Many of the issues the Israelites faced in the desert are relevant to issues of today.)

Before I go forward, the Israelites had seen God show his miraculous glory. While in Egypt, boils and sores fell on the Egyptians—not on the Israelites. *(Exodus: 9:10)* Hail fell and destroyed the crops and cattle in Egypt, but there was no hail in Goshen. *(Exodus 9:18-27)* Darkness fell over Egypt for three days. It was so dark you couldn't leave the house. Now that's darker than any country road in Alabama at night. Even though it was dark as midnight in Egypt in the daytime, Goshen (the Israelites' land) had sunshine. *(Exodus: 10:22-23)* While they were in the desert, (manna) or bread fell from the sky six days a week. *(Exodus 16:4)* And all the years they spent in the desert, their clothes didn't wear away. *(Deut: 29:5)* Man, even the baby's clothes grew with the baby.

After witnessing all of God's miraculous works, the Israelites still didn't believe God was capable of delivering the seven foot tribe's land into their hands.

God took Israel out of Egypt. But, why couldn't He take Egypt out of the Israelites?

Today, we'd say it like this: you can take the people out of the ghetto, but, can you really take the ghetto out of the people?

Every Black man and woman in America knows our history. In our time of slavery, our men were stripped of their manhood, fatherhood and dignity. Our women were treated in the same manor. However, our women had an extra trial to deal with—such as being taken sexually without consent.

Although Black America has been free for over a century, many of the idiosyncrasies of slavery exist today.

The greatest problem with the Israelites is they were physically rescued from slavery. However, mental slavery was alive and well within them.

Many of our brothers and sisters are physically free from slavery, but not mentally free.

Most Americans tend to think that there's one type of slavery and it only existed in our country's past. The truth is; there are many types of slavery, and slavery still exists today.

For example: I read a survey once that stated fifty percent of Americans are not happy with their current occupation and twenty-five percent of the American work force shows up just for the paycheck.

There are only 8,760 hours in a year. At the extreme minimum of the full time job schedule, we spend 1,952 hours (big holidays' time excluded) on the job.

However, everyone knows that to make it in today's world, forty hours a week will not cut it, but let's roll with the minimum.

Factor in dress time (1 hour) and commuting time (30 min). That's another 488 hours. Almost thirty percent (27.85%) of the year's time is devoted to indirectly and directly to work.

One third of the year's time is spent on preparing, commuting to, working on, and commuting from a job that you cannot stand. Nearly one third of your life force is spent in asking, "Would you like fries with that shake?" I know very well that you'd like to tell them were to stick them fries.

Now, tell me. Is working somewhere for forty plus hours a week and hating every minute of it a form of slavery?

The underlying factor in working a hated job is fear. The fear of a new risk or challenge keeps many people in job bondage.

I'd like to present two states of mind. Either one of these mindsets can be operating within us unbeknownst. The mindsets I'm referring to are of freedom and slave. If we are not careful, a slave mindset will occupy our thinking and cause us to make decisions from a slave's point of view.

I find it very challenging to be around people with slave mentality.

Why? People, of a slave mentality, take each and everyday as they come. Slaves don't make waves. They go with the flow. Whatever the master gives them for the day is the acceptable lot of the day. Slaves have no plans for their lives. Their master holds the keys to their future. Slaves don't decide where or what they'll have to eat. The master has got that covered. Slaves don't plan or plot to find a suitable mate. The master selects when and who they will breed with. And if they want to marry, they need the master's blessing.

Slaves don't plan for their children's future; the master will keep some and sell some.

Slaves lead purposeless lives. On second thought, slaves carry-out the purposes of other people.

Having been raised by a single divorced mother with four siblings, no one can honestly tell me that having children by a man that's not your husband is not a form of slavery. When a man shirks his responsibility for his children, the mother is most times destine to a life of poverty, insurmountable internal and external conflict, and loneliness to name a few. Tell me that's not a form of slavery.

There is a high contrast in regards to the two mentalities.

Free people take the time to make key life decisions early on in life. Planning and plotting is always on the top of the agenda.

Slaves never take directional authority over their lives.

Free people take the time to evaluate life and the possibilities that life has to offer. Then they take action and head towards those possibilities.

Slaves look at opportunities as a disruption of the comfortable and predictable life. "What I got isn't what I want, but hey, I'm surviving."

Free people keep watch over the distractions and pit falls of life. Free people don't have time to live out every one of life's mistakes. They learn from the mistakes of others.

Slaves go into the ditches of life head first.

Free people take the time to consider the next generation that will come from their loins. "What type of life do I want my children to have? Where will they go to school and college? What type of man or woman do I want them to marry? How can I make an impact on my grandchildren's lives?"

Slaves reproduce at will and never give a second thought on the child's or children's futures. Slaves leave their children to fend for themselves like wild animals.

Free people are always looking for ways to better themselves and their immediate environment.

Slaves only care about themselves and the events of today. After all, if tomorrow will be like today, why should the slave care about today or tomorrow for that matter?

Free people exercise discipline and courage.

Slaves cast off restraints and fear everything outside of the master's scope of thinking.

In a sense, many Black Americans have taken a slave mentality in regards to our families. Many times, as teens and young adults, we fail to plan for our families. As you've all heard the statement, fail to plan—plan to fail.

It's not so much that we're deliberately neglecting our families. I don't think that the importance of a traditional family is really understood. Because most of us are not brought up in the two parent environment, we don't see the great possibilities with two parents at the helm of the family. Traditional family ignorance has cost us great strides in the American dream.

If I can express what's most important about the two mentalities, the most important is to not let your parents' or past life experiences dictate the future—not to let slave mentality rule.

Look around. Slave mentality in regards to our families is alive and well. As Black Americans, we can't possibly be planning our future or lives—not with the premarital pregnancy statistics of today.

Don't be a victim of slave mentality. Don't be a distributor of slave mentality. Plan your life while you're young. Write down the things you'd like to accomplish. Set a time for marriage and children. Most likely, you'll pass the time set for marriage (I passed my set time.), but plan the time anyway. It's better to be a little bit off the planned schedule than to have no plan at all.

Discover your life's purpose as early as you can. Set your goals and objectives around that purpose, and stick to your plans.

A sixteen year old girl does not need a boyfriend. For what? What is the purpose of a sixteen year old girl having a boyfriend? Is she going to marry soon? Can she and her boyfriend afford to rent an apartment and pay utility bills? Can she feed herself and her man with meals other than from fast food restaurants? Are she and her boyfriend prepared to be parents? If she's answered "no" to any one of these questions, she needs to let that boy go and not date until the appropriate time.

The purpose for dating is for it to lead to marriage. A sixteen year old girl is not ready for any of that. So, why is she dating? Is it for pre-marital sex? Is it for pregnancy? Is it to catch a sexually transmitted disease?

Don't be a slave to your peers—always be a free individual.

Our communities (Black America) need more men and women to have a clear plan for the next generation. Our communities need people who are thinkers and innovators. Our communities need people like our mothers and fathers of the twenties, thirties, forties, fifties and sixties that looked ahead for the next generation and made the necessary sacrifices to change the future.

These achievements cannot be accomplished with "slave mentality." In fact, accomplishing future changes will never be done by a people with slave mentality.

When a man is not interested in marrying you or in marriage in general, but very interested in getting the desserts from you, he's operating with slave mentality. When a man won't take the time to educate himself to make himself more of a marriage candidate, he's operating in a slave mentality.

Hook up with any of these types of men, even if you have the mind of a free person, eventually you'll be converted into a slave.

Life is like a train. It takes a while to get the wheels moving. It takes a while to start moving down the tracks. It takes a while to reach your intended destination.

In the beginning of life, before the life train starts moving (before the end of high school), decisions must be made on what type of life you will live. One of the key questions you must ask yourself is: when will I start having sex? Believe it or not, sexual choices have brought many men and women to destinations that were never on his or her itinerary. No one is looking to die early from AIDS. No one is looking to get pregnant before finishing the tenth grade.

A hidden drive lies in us all. All of us want to see the next generation do better than we've done. In the early years of life, make plans for your intended children. One of the ways you can help your children do better than you is to have two full-time parents.

Even if your finances cannot send your children to one of the top ten colleges in America or put them in a seven bedroom home, the best gifts that can ever be given to our children are manhood and womanhood. Those gifts require the effort of both mom and dad— together or estranged.

Parents (single, married, divorced or widowed) should talk to their children about marriage and its benefits— even if marriage didn't work out for you.

Parents should encourage their children to think about their futures. Parents should empower their children to dream and plan their futures.

I think that many adults and children don't realize the power they have over their own lives. The power of decision is the greatest power one can have—especially when used properly and not abused.

God has given all of us "free will." He placed the tree of knowledge of good and evil in the garden and gave the command not to eat of it. Because of "free will," Adam and Eve ate of the tree. It wouldn't have been such a big deal if God had put Angels around the tree to block Adam and Eve from eating of it. They would've simply stayed away. But He gave Adam and Eve "free will" to eat and didn't interfere with the gift of decision.

God gave them the ability to choose what direction their lives would go, and they chose to eat—hence the plight of mankind.

It is always to your benefit to pick or choose plan "A" before plan "B" picks you. Plan "B" is the place of indecision. I would rather be calling the shots as a free man than to have a slave master stick me with plan "B".

Be free. Decide how your life will be before someone else sticks you with their plan.

Money

We've talked about the Black man's lack of money. Not all brothers are broke. Many handle their family matters well. Now, let's discuss the flip side of lack of cash. Let's talk about the sisters' financial habits.

A few years back, I went over my sister's home. She answered the door and told my wife, children and me to come back in the bedroom. She was in a middle of a project.

I walked in her room to find the contents of her walk in closet all over her master bedroom.

"What are you doing?" I asked.

"I'm sorting out my shoes," she replied.

Then, she picked up a *Polaroid* camera and snapped a picture of a shoe that was perfectly set on top of its box.

I started laughing and asked again, "what are you doing?"

She looked at me and started laughing.

"I can never find the shoe I want when I want it, because I cannot remember what's inside the box," my sister informed.

I started hollering with laughter and so did my wife.

My sister was taking pictures of her shoes so she could place the picture on the outside of the box—all so she wouldn't have to wreck the stack or go through all of the boxes until she found the shoe of her liking.

Now, the picture taking is solving a problem. However another hidden problem exists.

I must give her credit for being ingenious in finding a solution to such a massive problem. I bet someone will use that solution.

However, if my sister only had five to ten pair of shoes, I don't think she'd be spending her entire Saturday with a *Polaroid* camera in her bedroom.

I estimate that she had anywhere from thirty to forty pairs of shoes. And believe me; I'm probably underestimating the actual count.

My sister has worked and acquired her CPA. She holds a Master's Degree in Business Administration. She worked her way up the ranks and has earned every thing she owns. Even though I think it was a waste of money, she could afford to have that many shoes. So who am I to intrude on her lifestyle?

There are two types of money handlers in the world— savers and spenders.

When I first got married, I was the S-P-E-N-D-E-R. I knew very well how to spend money.

My wife was the budgeter or the saver. She knew how to save for emergencies and plan for the future.

The greatest obstacle with money for individuals is not the quantity of cash—but quality of its use.

The next time a nice sum of money comes your way, watch your actions.

If the ink hasn't dried on the check and you're at the mall before you get the cash, you're a spender.

If you run down to the bank to deposit the check in your savings account, you're a saver.

Spending and savings habits will let you know if you're wasting your time playing the lottery. If you hit the lottery for ten million dollars and love to spend money, you'll be back on someone's job before your life is over. Why? You can't wait to spend. You live to spend. If I were you, I wouldn't waste my time playing the lottery. You'll be broke again, unless you change your mindset.

Most people who have the discipline to save their money don't play the lottery. Why not? I can put my five dollars in the bank and almost for certain come back for the same five dollars with a little extra added to it. Lotteries never give refunds if you loose. Those five dollars per day given to the lottery game is $35 per week which translates to $1,820 per year. That's a nice vacation for a single person, or better yet, that can kill the balance on a credit card.

Savers are continuously calculating the cost to benefit ratio.

In marriage, usually opposites attract. A spender and saver will usually wed, and that's a good mix.

Sometimes, a little spending is necessary, but all of the time saving is an absolute must. The two spouses will balance each other out.

When two spenders are joined in Holy matrimony and one or both of the spenders over spend and/or mismanages the cash, that is when the bickering and "Yo Momma," arguments start.

When two savers get together another catastrophe is awaiting birth. If both of the newlyweds are tighter than panty hose two sizes small, hoarding from the other is highly possible. That is just as bad as the spenders, because in both cases (over spending and hoarding), selfishness is the captain. Marriages never last with that kind of partnership.

Today, many American marriages are financially lopsided. The unbalanced scales are highly prevalent in our community. Many Black American females are bringing home the cheddar and slicing it with an electric slicer.

When the woman makes as much as two thirds of the cash flowing into the home; usually she is in charge of the finances.

When the husband blows his third on the way home from work or doesn't show up to work for his third, that's when the problems escalate.

Notice I said escalate. The financial problems begin at the start, when the man is unable to carry his fair share of the financial load.

Women say that they are fine with carrying the majority of the load. However, let the man's mistakes or mismanagement cost her a good portion of her financial cheddar. She'll remind him, "I bring the cheese home in this house."

Most women have an innate desire to be cared for. That desire is a gift from God. This need is almost always neglected when she is the chief bread winner.

However, the flip side to the lopsided financial equation is when the man is the chief bread winner and he comes home to find a thousand dollar dress in the closet instead of the groceries for the month.

Or better yet, he comes home to find his kids wrapped in towels for diapers because she blew the diaper money on lottery tickets.

Black men and women alike need to learn to discipline themselves in regards to their cash flow.

Over the years, I've learned a financial principle; it's not how much you earn, it's how much you keep.

I've learned another principle by observation, more money will not solve the problem of being a financial idiot—which I once was. Financial troubles are all relative. If you earn ten thousand dollars a year and mismanage it, you'll mismanage the one hundred thousand dollars a year in earnings also. The only consequences that more money provides are bigger mistakes.

Out of all the industrialized countries in the world, America saves the least amount of their earned income.

That's sad, because around fifty percent of the American workers hate their job—which means there are millions of trapped American workers out there.

I've heard it reported that most Americans are spending $1.25 for every dollar earned. We all know that Uncle Sam and our lovely states must get their fourteen to thirty-three cent tip on every dollar earned. So, that leaves us with an approximate net of 67 to 86 cents per dollar earned. Now, if we are spending $1.25 for every dollar earned, we are falling into a financial pit, and only God will be able to help us get out.

I know you must know where the extra money is coming from. As the Federal Government borrows to cover its debt; so does the American citizens.

If it were impossible to earn enough money in the United States to meet the essentials like food, water, shelter, basic clothing, I guess over spending would probably be justifiable. That, however, is not the case. Most of America's over spending is due to over indulgence and/or keeping up with Mr. and Mrs. Jenkins.

During my lifetime, I've seen countless women give away articles of clothing with the price tags still affixed. I've seen men trade in perfectly good twelve to twenty-four month old cars all because a newer, bigger, and/or faster model was desired or came on the scene. I've seen televisions of epic proportions find their way into the smallest of dwelling places.

A few years ago, I went over a friend of a friend's house. The apartment was so small that I couldn't get far enough back from the television to get a good view of the program I was watching. The television was so big that the owner had to position it at an angle, because it was longer than the back wall in the living room of the apartment. Why didn't they save the television money for a down payment on a home?

Money is like sex—we all want some. And just like sex, we all want more money than we're getting.

The real test of a financially responsible disciplined individual is; what he or she does with the right now money once obtained.

Over spenders come in all genders, shapes and sizes. Myself included, I've seen many men over spend. On one of my former jobs, I knew a guy that had a boat, two new cars, a giant mortgage payment, a stay at home wife and three children. To add to the financial burden, half of his commute to work was over fifty miles.

I knew another guy at my most recent employment that is in way over his head. He likes cars. He owns a Hummer, late model Corvette and late model Dodge Viper. To support his posh cravings for expensive vehicles, he works every hour of overtime offered on the job—four extra hours a night and eight hours on Saturday. When the company cut the overtime, his colleagues speculated that they'd find him hanging off of the roof at work. His colleagues expected him to crack under the extremely large financial bricks he placed himself under.

Credit card companies are a trip. The companies will extend credit to any high risk person.

At the risk of sounding elementary, credit card companies make their money when its customers carry a balance.

Think about it. I give you five thousand dollars in credit. If I charge you ten percent per year, at the end of the twelve month period, I've earned approximately five hundred dollars on my five thousand just by letting you use my money. And in addition to the five hundred dollars in interest, you still owe me my initial five thousand dollars.

Now, secondly, I design a payment system that will keep you paying on that five thousand dollars for about thirty years—providing no additional purchases are made.

We all know that our balances will not stop at five thousand dollars, unless that is our credit limit.

Think about giving away approximately five hundred dollars a year. If the minimum payment of $43.88 per month is made, thirty years later, you will have given the credit card company $10,796.29. As you can see, that is over double the initial amount borrowed. And, I used a favorable interest rate of ten percent. I've seen interest rates close to thirty percent (close to thirty cents per year on every dollar borrowed).

Over the years, I've learned that as an American citizen, I have the same rights to compounding interest as the credit card companies. If I lend some investigation time to the compounding interest project, suitable investments can be found, so that I've turned my five thousand initial investment into $10,796.29. And the best part of that deal, your name and social security number will be on the statement when it arrives at your dwelling place—not Bank so and so.

When I was a kid, I saw the use of credit cards, but I never saw what the statement looked like. I never saw the interest charges the companies charged. I never saw my Mom paying the credit cards either.

We were financially challenged most of the month, because we were on welfare.

Anyone who has been through the welfare system knows that the Government does not want you living the life of Riley. They keep the funds tight and practically make you beg for the extras. They make sure you always have a need.

I always viewed credit cards as a way of doing what I could not do on my own—SUPER PLASTIC.

When I became depressed because I had no money, I'd go to the stores with my cards and use plastic power.

God knows, if I didn't have any extra cash in my pocket, I shouldn't have been in the mall.

Needless to say, my irresponsibility caused me to dig a neck-high grave for myself and when all my discretionary cash was all gone, my creditors pushed me into the grave that I dug for myself.

And I asked myself, "How could they?"

I thought the credit card companies were my friends. They always called me "Mr. Childress" when I called to get my limit raised. I thought they loved me.

I found out how much love they had for me the first time I couldn't meet the minimum payment. The same credit card companies that called me "Mr. Childress" began filling the hole with water, all while I struggled to get out of my neck-high grave. The credit card companies' venomous fangs were exposed when they realized that they were not getting their initial capital back.

They were in the lending business to make money— not to make me feel like someone important—not to help me find happiness in the latest gadget.

The credit card companies were just as at fault as I was. They were feeding me steak when they knew I could only afford hot dogs and beans.

Not to use the credit card companies as an escape goat—however, the problem was a cooperative effort. I was still receiving credit card offers in the mail—even after I was clearly in trouble. Because I was having trouble meeting all my minimums, I'd get a new card to shuffle money around—robbing Peter to pay Paul (using the cash advance checks from the new credit card to pay other credit card payments). Boy was I in there.

I gave the creditors access to my credit report so I could obtain credit. They could see the risk and...the inevitable. Even while in my neck-high grave, credit was still being extended to me. And it wasn't five or seven hundred dollars of credit. It was more like 5 to 7 g's of credit.

Money is the number one reason why many marriages fail.

Many single people that desire to marry don't realize that the other woman or man (excuse my language) ain't got nothing on the big boy of marriage failure, and that big boy is money.

Money issues are still taking out more marriages than infidelity.

The money fights, in early marriage, mostly come from the lack of financial knowledge by one or both individuals, competition, complacency, power struggles and/or the supply of cash into the household—be it in excess or in pittance.

I know this first hand, because when I got married, I was heavily loaded with debt. I didn't realize how much of a hindrance debt was on a new relationship, until it was too late.

When I got married, we lived in an apartment. Not long after we married, our first child was born. We wanted more children, so the one bedroom apartment wouldn't work. We needed a house.

I was so loaded with debt that I had to purchase a handy-man's special. It was all we could afford. I thank God for the experience, but there's nothing like purchasing a home and moving right in—no cosmetic work to be done.

I could've kicked myself, because I made plenty of money to save for a home—but I didn't. I wasted my single years having "fun."

It's good to enjoy life. It's good to have fun, but while you're having fun, don't forget to plan for your future.

Save and invest your money.

Single people are in more debt then ever before in our history. Many women are waiting for "Mister Right" to bail them out of financial troubles. That is unfair. He didn't create the debt, nor should he be responsible for rescuing you.

In the book, *"The Millionaire Next Door,"* by Thomas J. Stanley and William D. Danko, a man was engaged to be married. He discovered how much debt his fiancé was carrying and decided that she was not the woman for him. Furthermore, he was very upset with her ways of deception. She didn't openly lie to him, but she never confided with him either. She thought that after the marriage he'd clean up her mess. She was so wrong.

It is never to anyone's benefit to run up massive debt. Sometimes it happens from illness or circumstances. But, for someone to go into debt deliberately is insane and thoughtless.

Straighten out your debt. Cut up the cards. Live under your means. If you make a dollar, tithe your 10 percent and live on $0.50 and save the rest. Establish yourself. Acquire assets that provide income, like a business, income producing dwelling places, stocks bonds, and royalties. Purchase depreciating assets with cash whenever possible.

Avoid purchasing excessive depreciating assets like, cars, televisions, clothes, etc.

Read books on money. I learned why I mismanaged my money. Truth be told. I learned what I learned about money from my Mom—hence my financial train wreck.

Black Americans have more money flowing through their hands now than ever before in history. We as a group are included in the marketing plans of many large corporations. They are now seeing the benefit in making commercials that appeal to us. Why? We've got earning power now. Don't be stupid with your money.

Don't be impressed with how much money your man makes. Be more impressed with what he does with the money he already has, because that will determine your financial future.

If he always has to have the latest and greatest, you'll be the wife of the man with the *Mercedes* parked in the parking lot of the apartment complex.

There is nothing wrong with owning a *Mercedes*. Just make sure you own a home or some property before the *Mercedes*.

Have your priorities in order—first things first.

Cha-Ching!!

Where are all my gold diggers at? Holler at your boy!

In my day, I ran into a few gold diggers—take me here, take me there, buy me this, and pay for that.

In one aspect, I respect the gold digger, because she never lets you forget what the relationship is all about. She is never ever phony. It is all about what I can get in the shortest amount of time.

If you ever want to make a man feel like an ATM with legs, start digging in his pockets before he gets to know you or you get to know him.

As I've told you before, men are driven to women. A man with a respected girl will do what ever he can to meet her needs.

This principle that most men live by has been abused by lots of women. The principle has been abused so much, that I will say it makes selling drugs and other illegal activities look more attractive to young impressionable men with wayward dreams.

Gold diggers make the possibilities of a good relationship impossible. Relationships have no room for selfish and callous individuals.

"You give me this and I'll give you that" is the foundation of the gold digger's relationship. Once he or she cannot give anymore, the relationship is over.

Having been dug out in a gold digging relationship, I always disliked the spirit of gold digging. I was not fooled by all the affection and attention. I knew that the day I could not fulfill my part of the contract, she would leave.

The gold digger made me feel more inhuman than any racist or racism that I encountered during normal life.

Leeches and parasites find hosts to live on. They will never leave so long as the host provides them with what they need (food & shelter). The minute the host dies or the source of food becomes unavailable, they detach and look for a new host.

The only way the host can get rid of leeches or parasites is to physically remove them or take medication that will kill the parasite. Incidentally, the medication is very dangerous for the host. Some parasites will only die from taking light doses of insecticides. Unfortunately, there are some ingested parasites that will stay with you until the grave.

Gold diggers have the same mentality as leeches and parasites. They don't make their own way, they use others to get what they want or need.

Is that all you want from your man? "Give me this and I'll give you that." Are cash, clothes, cars and diamonds that important? Don't you know that he is a human being with feelings?

Most men will not tolerate a gold digger. Those that do, eventually tire from the pressure and constant badgering.

There is more to life then what you wear, where you live and what you drive. These material things are like vapor in the wind—they pass.

If you are a gold digger, you need to repent and never go back to digging. Set some goals for yourself, and you'll see how hard most people work to accomplish what they have. After accomplishing a few goals for yourself, you'll have mad respect for anyone that has accomplished anything, and gold digging will become a thing of the past.

Never let your friends influence your decisions of a lifetime!

Ladies, the deck is not stacked in your favor. Cut out the games and be ready for Mr. Right when he shows up. You cannot waste any time with your heart being tied up with someone that's not marrying material.

While I was writing this book, I ran into an old female friend of mine.

My two year old took off running in the mall as she did on many occasions. While moving swiftly to catch up with her, my old friend caught my eye. Of course I paused for a minute to recognize, because it had been over fourteen years since I'd seen her.

Honestly, I checked her out briefly. I was surprised to see that she looked almost the same way she did fourteen years ago. She hadn't gained any significant weight nor did she let her other features; like hair, skin, etc., deteriorate and she was still attractive.

Of course you know that I looked at her ring finger. She had absolutely no rings on her fingers. Yes, I checked her ring finger again. It was as bare as a freshly shaved bald head.

At one time in my life, I lived in the Vailsburg section of Newark, NJ. At the time, living in Vailsburg wasn't quite as bad as living on Muhammad Ali Blvd in Newark. But it was Newark just the same.

I met my old friend in the neighborhood. She lived right across the street from me.

In the summer of 1989, everybody on the block stayed out late. I didn't stay out too late, because I had a job. I got to know her by chillin' with the crew. I liked her a lot, but she had a chump of a boyfriend—no job—no car—younger than her—lived at home with Momma. I couldn't believe she would go out with a guy like that.

Her boyfriend of the time claimed to be disabled because of a fight he had at a trade school. Someone hit him in the eye with a padlock. I could accept him being home all day because he was disabled from the altercation. The problem I had with her boyfriend was every time someone had beer or alcohol he could see the bottle from a distance. If he could see that good, he needed to be working.

Plus I had a girlfriend. But, she was just something to do. I had no plans on *ever* marrying her. She was breaking off the brownie and I was taking it.

(Please note that I am a Christian now, and even though I was a fornicator, I do not condone fornication and/or adultery. The Bible states; flee from fornication. When I fornicated, I knew it was wrong and did it anyway. Fornication was wrong then and is still wrong today.)

Believe it or not, my girlfriend and her boyfriend were cousins.

I saw some qualities in her that were in sharp contrast to the relationship she was in. Although my friend lived home with her mother (more acceptable for women than men), she drove a brand new car. She had a decent office job with the state government. Plus, she was really easy to look at.

I invited her out for a weekend down at the Jersey shore. She accepted.

We had a great weekend. I really got to know her.

I know this might be hard to believe, but we didn't have sex. *Yes*, the opportunity definitely presented itself, but I didn't take it.

Why didn't I have sex with her?

I was ready to settle down. I really liked the girl and I thought we could get to know each other before exchanging desserts. So, sex wasn't my highest priority for the weekend.

(When a man is really interested in you, he'll be just as interested in what you have to offer outside of the bedroom as well as inside the bedroom.)

We came back from our weekend and the *snitzle* hit the fan. Her boyfriend put two and two together and realized that we had snuck away for the weekend.

What a week of arguing and fussing that followed. I couldn't believe the drama that unfolded. I had drama coming from my so-called girlfriend. I had the most drama coming from her boyfriend. I was hoping and waiting for someone...anyone to throw a fist at me. I would've made sure that it was regretted.

After all the dust cleared, she decided to go back to her boyfriend.

I was hurt. But I decided to release her from my pursuit.

I was also disappointed. I couldn't believe that the haters had that much influence on her. If she couldn't make decisions independent from her friends, what kind of wife would she make?

I, on the other hand, was really totally finished with my girlfriend. After I sat in front of my building and cursed all of them out, I went upstairs to my mother's apartment, laid across my bed and begin to mentally sever all ties to my girlfriend and my intended girlfriend.

Two years later in May of 1991, I moved out of my mother's apartment into my own.

I met my wife in August of the same year.

One evening in October or November, my phone rang. My wife (which was my girlfriend at the time) picked up the phone. You know who it was right?

We talked briefly, and I told her I had a girlfriend. The conversation stalled briefly and she asked, "The girl that answered the phone?"

"Yeah," I replied.

When I got ready to get off of the phone, my wife said, "Let me have the phone please."

I gave it to her.

"Hello, what's your name?" My future wife kindly asked.

She answered.

"Irv and I have been dating for a little while now, so I suggest you loose his phone number."

I chuckled and returned to my activity in the kitchen. My old intended girlfriend was a day late and a dollar short. I already moved on.

(If I were not ready for marriage, I would've never let my girl have the phone.)

That was the last time I'd heard from her until our brief encounter at the mall.

During the span of time called life, you will have people that are passing through (insignificant) and those that are gems (significant).

What ever you do in this short time span called life, never let people passing through your life, influence the major decisions of life.

'Hood drama' stole a real opportunity from this girl. I can't say if we would've ever married, but all possibilities for it to happen were snuffed out the day I cussed everybody out.

When working on securing your spouse, don't let the other crabs in the barrel influence your decision or let them know what you're trying to accomplish.

The building where I lived in Vailsburg is gone just like the possible relationship that could've grown out of it. Fire took the building and her friends took our possibility.

Believe it or not, the world is full of haters. The haters do not want you to be happy at all. Soap opera drama is built on haters (jealous people).

Please focus and recognize a good man while the opportunity is in front of you. Don't let haters rob you of your possibilities or destiny.

Believe me when I tell you, haters can see the potential that exists in your life. That's why they are determined to stop the progress. The hater wants what you have. The hater fears that they will never get what you have, so if the hater cannot be happy, he or she will make sure you are not happy.

The hater only succeeds when you give in or give up.

Always remember, life is forever changing. The people in your life today will most likely not be in your life tomorrow. Remember that when people are advising you on "what to do with your life's decisions." Most likely, that person or persons will be nowhere to be found when you are suffering the consequences.

It's a Black Thing!

Recently, Hollywood released a film called "*Something New*." The film seemed like it was targeted to African American females in their prime years for marriage. The lead character in the film was a successful Black American woman struggling to find a good Black man. As it happened, she fell in love with a white landscaper. And of course at the end of the movie she married the man—sorry for those of you that did not see it.

The movie tanked at the box office. Apparently, Hollywood did not check the stats or get the memo about black women. Most Black women want a Black man. Most black women are not willing to cross ethical, cultural, and/or racial lines to get a decent man. I don't believe that our women make this choice with racism at the root of the decision. I believe that Black women prefer to marry someone that looks like and comes from a similar background as they do.

There is nothing wrong with desiring someone that is similar to you in many ways. There is a problem when a man or woman says, "I will never marry a..." and a racial slur fills in the blank. That's full blown racism no matter which race it comes from. I've met just as many Black racists as I've met white ones. The problem with the decision is: Most Black women have limited themselves to the ways of Black men (the exceptional, the good, the bad and the ugly). Most of the time, the options are very limited.

In this country, crossing racial lines to marry is always a controversial move. The controversy emanates from the couple's family and from society. Many interracial marriages fail because one or both spouses lose relationships with key family members like a parent. Add the pressure from society's gawks, and not so pleasant comments, and you have a recipe for destruction or in today's vernacular—divorce. Finding someone to spend the rest of your life with is no easy challenge inside or outside of your race.

Quite frankly, many Black women believe that they are good women. The term "good woman" has many different meanings to many different women. All of the women I've dated in the past, and I can say all, were good women to a certain degree—some more than others. However, honestly, they were not good enough for me to marry—sorry.

Good people come in all shapes, colors and sizes. Bad people come in all shapes, colors and sizes. Happiness and love are color blind. After living with my wife of fourteen years, I can say with all honesty, if you have a shot at happiness with someone that does not look like you, take it. Take it! I think about all of the good days with my wife and even the not so good days. It is worth it all. What is the "it" in the previous sentence? It is happiness and love! Happiness and love are very expensive and rare commodities when dealing with the opposite sex. If you happen to find it with someone that doesn't look like you or come from where you come from, so what! Anyone in your circle that cannot understand the principles of happiness and love probably does not deserve to be in your circle—including family members.

When I met my wife, I was going through some challenges with my mother. I was tempted to break it off with my future wife so that I could give the care to Mom that she needed. I heard the voice of God as clear as day. He said, "Irv, if you break up with your girlfriend to take care of your mother, it will be a very long time before someone of marrying caliber comes along." Never make a long term decision based on today's circumstances. I took heed to the wisdom of God and kept my girlfriend—future spouse. And believe it or not, the problem that my Mom had with her living quarters was worked out in the weeks that followed the Word from the Lord. Two years, later my girlfriend and I tied the knot. One year after that, Mom passed away. Had I done what I thought was best, I would've had no wife and no mother in three years time. Be careful who you are listening to—even when the information seems like it will work for the current situation. Most times in life, you'll be given an opportunity at an inopportune time. Had I listened to the fears of the time, I would've missed out on happiness and love.

Great love and happiness are not promised to come in the desired package. Don't ever shun a person because he or she is not covered with your desired skin color. Don't let other insignificant people's opinions drive you away from love and happiness. Everyone on God's green earth has one mother and one father (Adam and Eve). Physically, all humans are generally the same. Never let physical appearance (color) be the reason for not giving a person that generally cares for you the time of day.

Plastic or Real

Cosmetic procedures are on the rise. The procedures are so popular that we have television shows about them. It's no surprise that women account for 90 percent of all cosmetic procedures. Why? It's pretty obvious. Most women are not happy with their bodies.

But something else can be derived from the stat. Women are increasingly spending more money on their outward appearance rather than their inward qualities.

Women are constantly being bombarded by commercials, videos, movies, television, etc. The messages sent from the various forms of media are always clear—big breast—small waist—curvy bottom—pouty lips.

Only in the last two years, have plus size models gained ground in the advertising industry.

Men are still acting like fools even with surgically enhanced women.

I'm not for or against plastic surgery. An excellent outward appearance always does the mind well. If I were given a ridiculous sum of cash, I'd have a couple of features that I'd really consider repairing. Of course, I think God would probably have a problem with me fixing his living and breathing soil, because, what God does is always beautiful.

Something has been lost in the new surgery age. Our generation is a microwave generation. We want everything right now and as quickly as possible. If you don't think that's true, next time you're in a fast food joint, check your blood pressure after waiting in line for more than five minutes.

While a good plastic surgeon can open the door of opportunity in regards to dating and progressing towards marriage, the surgeon is limited to only repairing or reconstruction physical features. He or she cannot repair the soul.

The best investment a woman can make in her life is in building her self-worth.

Enlarging your breast and/or taking off the extra giggly parts of your body can never fix a woman whose soul is empty.

When your cup is empty, you have nothing to offer, because emotionally you are bankrupt. The people in your circle (including your man) may have to walk away from their investment in you, because you've mismanaged it with poor esteem.

Do you really think bigger boobs can make you more dateable and/or closer to being marriage material? If a man finds a woman with big fun bags, and that's all she has to offer, he'll stay for the fun of it.

Bigger breast and/or a round behind will definitely get you noticed and give you more dating options, but internal qualities will keep you in the game, long after everything perky becomes droopy.

The inner qualities of a woman are worth far more then anything she owns physically.

If you're willing to spend over $5,000 on a surgical procedure, you should be equally willing to invest double the money and time to make sure your internal vessel is filled. A woman with a full inner vessel has much more to offer a man. A full cupped woman is just one of the fringe benefits. The man gets a great mind and body.

Everyone knows, you can spend 10 grand on surgery and not be happy with the results—thus beginning a cycle of never ending repair.

Make sure you spend as much time as possible repairing the damage that daddy, other boyfriends, momma, auntie and anyone else that has been a hindrance. If you are dating, I recommend that you stop dating so your wounds can heal.

Believe it or not, a corrected and perfected inner being will out perform any set of fake ta-tas in the long run. In fact, in long term group situations, inner qualities will get you a leg up on the competition.

Women need to spend more time and effort on the inward rather than on the outward person. Women need to be able to entice a man with her mind as well as her body. Her body is the grand gift given to him after he's proven that he loves her as a whole person—not just a sexual play toy.

The Heavyweights

In 2006, my wife and I took our family on a vacation to a beautiful beach resort in the Carolinas. It was our first time at the beach. We had a ball. Just as it is at the Jersey shore, we had lots of things to do and places to visit. The resort's beaches were clean and the water was nice and warm. And, unlike the Jersey shore, the hotels were right on the beach. I liked that.

However, during the vacation, my wife and I couldn't help but notice the quite obvious. There were an awful lot of overweight people at the beach. And what made me chuckle was the lack of couth exhibited by the vacationers. Bikinis with bellies and oversized backsides were the "norm" when visiting the pool or the beach.

And the men—I've never seen so many pregnant men in one location in my entire life.

We finally found the vacation spot for the average American family.

One evening at dinner time, we left our accommodations for the buffet restaurant of our choice. We were on vacation in a city built around tourist. We got in the car and made a right turn and another right turn—all in less than a mile.

163

The second right turn proved to be difficult. We hit a traffic jam. How could we hit traffic in a vacation resort? Well, at the time we didn't realize it, but it was dinner time and the main drag I turned on was called *"Restaurant Row."* The traffic jam was from all of the tourists trying to get to the restaurant of choice. I couldn't believe it.

Earlier on our vacation when we were in a store, I asked what the sales tax was. The lady told me that the sales tax was five percent—less than Jersey's six percent at the time. I was pleased with that.

After our dinner, I got the bill for our feast. (Yeah, I'm not going to act like I wasn't putting down my fair share of edibles.) When I looked at my bill from the establishment, I noticed the 7.5% tax on the bill. I called it the "Fat Tax." At that moment, it occurred to me that the Carolina state had already been benefiting from my recent observations. The beach's state government was capitalizing on the "gotta eat" syndrome.

Not for nothing but, I plan to return to the resort town frequently, because it was one of the best vacations of my life. And the food was off the hook. (Yeah, I still like to eat.)

In the video *"Super Size Me"* Morgan Spurlock stated, "America has been labeled "The Fattest Country." I've been looking around in several different states and I'm beginning to believe that this statement is a true one.

I would do an injustice to women by penning this book and not discussing weight.

Now, I know this subject is a touchy one. But at the risk of loosing a few friends, I'm going to tread the waters lightly.

I've always had a weight issue, and—if the truth be told—most people in this country are challenged in the area of weight. I've been blessed, because at my heaviest I was sixty-five pounds overweight.

My aunt was not so lucky. At one time in her short life (43 years), she had surpassed the five hundred pound mark. So with that said, I understand that there is more to weight than diet and exercise. Brain function, endocrine system, metabolism and hormones also play an important part in weight.

Before I met my wife, I went to the gym four to five days a week. In three years' time, I gained much muscle and weighed about two hundred-five pounds. I was solid.

My only dream was to get the six pack. I never made it past my two pack.

When I first got my apartment, many times loneliness would set in. I had the *Domino's Pizza* joint on speed dial. And in the heat of depression, I called my friends with the big oven.

The doorbell rang. It was the man with my drugs...I mean pizza. Shortly after he left, I shoved the entire medium sausage pizza down the gullet along with a quart of sweetened iced tea.

I was still depressed, but for some reason the full tank made me feel a little better about being alone.

Of course the next day, I'd feel real guilty and punish myself at the gym. If it weren't for the gym, I would've blown up.

A few months later, I met my wife and stopped going to the gym. Twenty-five pounds came out of the bushes and grabbed me.

I fluctuated with the twenty-five pounds for a few years, until my business was failing. Then I tipped the scales with sixty-five extra pounds.

I was really active at work (climbing ladders, pulling tools on to roofs, and working long hours). I believe that's what saved me from getting too heavy, because I was really over eating. At dinner time, I'd have four fried pork chops, candied yams, a vegetable made with butter and/or sugar, and drink almost two quarts of *Kool-Aid.* (We made the real *Kool-Aid* in the small packets that required real sugar to be added.) I should've recognized my problem when we were making a gallon of *Kool-Aid* for dinner and two-thirds of it was gone by the end of dinner. Both my wife and I gained a large amount of weight over time, and we really didn't notice it.

My wife has been really kind to me in regards to her weight. After our first child, she weighed less than she did before she got pregnant. After my son was born, we ran into business troubles. Both of us blew up. But even when my wife tacked on four sizes, I still wanted it. The key word in the previous sentence is "wife."

I noticed my patterns or cycles for weight fluctuations. Usually, I could link foul emotions to my over eating. The period of time when I struggled with my business was the most stressful and depressing time of my life, and I had three chins to prove it.

A man will show more tolerance for excessive weight with his wife than with the girl he's dating or intending to marry.

"A man has to accept me the way I am."

Most of the time, being over weight and depressed simultaneously won't afford you the luxury of finding Mr. Right.

Men are attracted by what they see. Because women in our communities are primarily raised by women, they're not afforded a man's perspective in regards to looks.

Any man that loves his daughter and desires grandchildren from her the legitimate way will speak the truth in love and kindness. He'd have no problem carefully telling his daughter to watch her portions. He'd have no problem with getting her involved in sports or some other type of physical activity.

Men are attracted by what they see. (I repeated this purposely.) That statement may sound harsh to some. However, it is what it is. It has always been this way. It won't ever change. Your feministic point of view will never change the way it is. If you desire a husband, you must change.

The weatherman can forecast rain, and almost everyone will accept his statements verbatim. And when it does rain, no one tries to stop the rain, because that is the way it is.

But, let a man tell women, "Men are attracted by what they see," and the women want to chew his head right off of his neck.

The truth to the matter is men are moved to action by what they see. If what they see does not attract them, they'll keep it moving.

I've heard the argument over weight issues on television, radio and with associates throughout the years. Ladies, you can argue this point until Jesus returns, but it still won't change the fact that men are attracted by what they see.

See. If you were to ask women what is the first thing they notice on a man, most will tell you, "his eyes." You'll never hear us men arguing that point. That's the woman's preference. That is what she likes. If my eyes are bloodshot with a yellowish tinge, I know my chances are slim to none with a female that likes nice eyes, and I'll keep it moving.

Women are not as visual orientated as men are— which explains why there are some ugly dudes with some fine women. Many women can and sometimes are swept off of their feet by the kindness and tenderness shown by the ugly man. See the ugly man understands this. Trust me; he's looked in the mirror many times over. He knows. That's why the flowers keep coming to your job. That's why you can count on him in the time of crisis. He goes the extra mile because of his feature challenges.

But if the same woman takes the one-sided woman's point of view (I like nice eyes. Facial features don't really matter. I like kindness. What the man looks like doesn't matter to me so long as he's good to me.), she'll get angry or defensive when a man says, "I'm not attracted to large women."

Men are not as in dept as you think we are. We lack the capacity and desire to dig deeper. One might have a great personality, but most men are not going to take the time to get past what the personality is packaged in. At the risk of being repetitive, men are attracted by what they see.

In my forty plus years on this planet, I've heard a lot of locker room talk in my home state of Jersey. If I've heard four men openly confess to desiring heavy women, that's a lot. It may be different down south and in other parts of the country.

I can remember two men distinctly and openly admitting that they liked their women pleasingly plump.

The one guy wasn't shamed at all. We were in eighth grade and a plump girl from our class left the room and he took a look at the extra large rump. He moaned, "Mmm, mmm, mmm!" Then, the entire class busted out in laughter. He didn't care either. He loves them like that. I still get a chuckle every time I think of it.

Although I've met a few, most African American men, in general, are not attracted to the twiggys that are seen on the 5th Ave runways. We like our women thick. We want every thing to look nice without too many exposed bones.

But at the same time, most African American men don't want a woman with excessive weight. We are simply not as attracted to larger women as proportionate women. Proportionate women are what we look for—not skinny—not fat—just right.

Being raised at home with Momma as the head of the household only gives most women a feministic view on the issues and facts of life. "A man has to accept me the way I am," is a feministic viewpoint. If out of the box thinking is not grasped quickly, the women with this view will have less of a chance of marrying simply because there aren't enough men out there that like larger women.

The question is not how shallow men are when it comes to physical appearance. The question is; do you want to conform to our way of thinking or not? Or better yet, how much is the statement, "A man has to accept me the way I am," worth to you? Is it worth possibly living your life without the man of your dreams?

A strong stance on that statement means you are willing to take the associated risk.

Here are a few tips for weight loss. First make a list of all items eaten in a day. Count your calories. After you've counted all calories, take note of how many calories are needed vs. how many calories are sipped and eaten. Reduce your calorie intake and increase your physical activity. Cut down on high fats and empty carbohydrates—like bacon, mayonnaise, soda, candy and chips. Stop eating at a certain time in the evening— like 7 pm. Dinner should be the smallest meal of the day. Why? After dinner, most people have a date with the couch and remote. Food's primary purpose is for nourishment and energy. If you have a date with the couch after a big meal, your body really has no use for the big meal you've just ingested. Forgo the burger and fries for a homemade salad. When eating salad; try to avoid the over supply of dressing. Some dressings have over 100 calories per tablespoon. I've seen people eating salads loaded with dressing and wondering why they are not loosing weight. One cannot loose weight if the salad contains as much as or even more calories as a regular plate of food. Some of the items on the salad bar are not fat free nor are they healthy items. Creamy sauces are to be avoided.

Don't go crazy dieting. When I was a gym regular, I was on my diet for five days a week. Saturday and

Sunday were my days off, and I enjoyed myself. If a break is not on the horizon, the diet will not last, because after all, telling me, "You can't have it," only makes me want it more. There has to be a couple days a week when caution can be thrown to the wind.

And finally, ladies what you do to get the man, you must do to keep him. Don't try to slim down to meet your man and then blow back up. You will have problems. Men marry what they want. If he wanted sixty or more extra pounds on you, that's the way he would've married you.

As part of your over all self improvement plan, diet and exercise should be a high priority. Women should never loose weight just to get a man—loose weight to keep yourself in good health and your options open. Do it because you are worth it to yourself—even if no one ever notices.

So you think you're in love?

I remember the love of my life. At least, that's who I thought Gina was, back in the day. I met her on my security officer job. I had never fallen in love before, until I met Gina. Gina was the girl that I lost three years of serious dating time.

At the time, I was twenty years of age—young and dumb on the subject of love.

Gina was the girl that I said the words, "I love you," to for the first time. And she did not disappoint me. When I revealed my love for her through spoken words, Gina reciprocated in like manner.

"I love you" from that special someone means different things to different people. For me, it meant my dreams and fantasies of being loved unconditionally by someone other than a family member had finally come true. The "I love you" meant my search for a wife was over, and I'd soon be on the road to being a parent. You see. The "I love you" meant I would somehow be repaid the missing love I missed as a child by Gina for all the years I spent in a divorced home.

As the relationship progressed, my dream became a nightmare. Gina and I were not heading down the aisle of matrimony. We were heading to splits-ville.

I'd make a date with the girl on Wednesday or Thursday for the coming Saturday night. Gina would agree to the date. I'd come to pick her up on Saturday. Her mother would answer the door and politely say, "Gina went out with her friend Jackie."

I'd be so embarrassed. Sometimes, (getting jerked on my dates was commonplace) it seemed as if Gina's mom wanted to give me a plate of greens and fried chicken as a consolation prize. On another occasion, I remember Gina's mom looking at the ground with shame as she stood in the doorway, because of Gina's repeated disregard for me.

I got stood up three out of four Saturdays.

I'd go to the mall with my siblings and see other girlfriends and boyfriends all hugged up and kissy kissy. I couldn't understand why my relationship wasn't like that, because that's what I desired most—to be wanted by someone special.

Even though, I was the only one in the relationship, that didn't stop me. I didn't want to take the time and read the hand writing on the wall. I didn't want to be honest with myself.

I figured if I yelled and screamed enough, she'd change her ways, and we could be the couple I desired us to be.

You cannot make someone do what they don't desire to do.

The more I fussed and cussed, the more I got jerked.

If I had any brains inside my head, I would've left before the brownies were dispersed. (I didn't get stood up all the time.)

Well it ended.

For the next four years, on any given week, I spent three to five days out of seven inside the liquor bottle trying to figure out why she did not love me like I loved her.

I wasted over four years of money and dating time, because my self-esteem was in the toilet. My relationship with Gina ran into trouble early on. If I had really loved myself, I would've been strong enough to walk away the first time she jerked me, but I feared nothing better would come along.

Well, someone better eventually came along and today I call her "MY WIFE."

Anyone can examine how much love they have for themselves in the beginning of a relationship. The first time a man slaps you across the face. The first time you find a suspicious number in his wallet or phone. The first time you find your man lying about money. Your reaction following the action determines your love for yourself.

If one is willing to tolerate lying, abuse and stealing—to name a few, you *ain't* got much love for yourself.

Fear and low self-esteem are a dangerous combination when dating. You'll never get the best that God has for you with those two numskulls in charge.

In the years preceding my wife, I began to drink less and finally deal with the hurt of the long gone relationship. As long as I drank, I never healed, and I anxiously waited for the day that Gina would return.

One evening, my phone rang after months of silence. It was Gina. We decided to get back together. I humbly re-submitted to being "The Stand-Up Guy." SIKE!

During my conversation with Gina, I had the pleasure of telling her that I was engaged. I haven't seen or heard from her since.

I've learned a lot from that relationship. If I can sum it up into one word, "desperate" comes to mind. Never be too desperate for a relationship to workout, bad or good.

I recommend that men and women spend some time in their adult years to figure themselves out. During the puberty years, your parents are pulling you in one direction. Your peers are pulling you in most likely the opposite direction of your parents. Spend some time developing yourself.

Towards the end of my drinking years, I began to travel. I found out how much I loved to travel. I began to find myself.

If you are a child of divorce or a child of a home with one parent missing, take some time to study yourself. Take some time to read books on family. But most of all, read books that are similar to the life you've lived.

I was fortunate enough to have been born in a family with Mom and Dad at the helm. But during my childhood, my dad left. I always tried to deny my need for my dad. I always tried to deny my need for healing. I always felt unloved. I know my mother and father loved me, but I felt unloved. That feeling stemmed from my father's sudden departure from the marriage. The more I denied it—the more un-loved Irv surfaced in subtle ways.

The biggest problem in the relationship with Gina was me and the lack of love I had for myself. If I had known what a real relationship looked like, I wouldn't have settled for the crumbs that I was getting.

If you are a child of divorce or have never seen one or both of your parents; please read books on family. Read the Bible. Find out what God says about family. He started it all. He knows how to fix it.

When you're looking for your spouse, look for him or her with your childhood wounds healed. If you enter the relationship with open sores, you'll bleed all over your future spouse. Some can take the sight of blood, but they'll do nothing about it—leaving you to fend for yourself in pain. Some, at the sight of blood, will help you close the wounds and get on with life. That ideal person comes along once or twice in life.

Others will see the work that needs to be done, be too weak at the sight of the blood and run like the wind—

you'll be divorced or alone repeating the generational cycle—be healed from the inside out.

Marriage is a business, and, like businesses only a few survive it for the long haul. In order to be successful at anything, time and effort must be put forth. No business has ever succeeded by accident. Deliberate and calculated moves drive a business to success.

The same is so with marriage. Deliberate and calculated moves will drive the marriage towards success. How can someone be successful at marriage if they didn't grow up in a home headed by marriage?

That is why some study time must be yielded to it. In the forties and fifties, most people were married and married for long periods of time. Most remarriages were due to the early passing of a spouse.

Women learned how to be wives by watching their mothers, grandmothers and aunts.

Men learned how to be husbands by watching their fathers, grandfathers and uncles.

Most marriages today are finished by the fifth to tenth year. So, who can you watch today? With no examples in our communities, we must read the Word of God first hand and get an understanding of the purpose of family. We must also seek the guidance of the older generation that is still married. Somehow, we must learn the purpose of marriage.

If we never learn the purpose of marriage, our families of tomorrow are doomed.

The Contract

Let's face it. Marriage is a business, and the contract or covenant is signed when you make your confession public—at the alter or in front of the judge.

A contract is a legal binding and enforceable by law.

When you stand at the alter or in front of the justice of the peace, not only are you bearing witness, you're one of the duly parties of that contract.

One great thing about a good contract is, should the other party break the contract or default, a dissolve of the contract is possible with both parties benefiting somewhat from the contract being signed before the relationship began.

We all watch the news. And we've all seen musical groups and solo artists in struggles with record companies, agents, etc.

I remember one female musical trio group. They declared bankruptcy after selling well over ten million copies of one CD release.

Part of the trio's bankruptcy stemmed from lack of financial savvy—the other was from not reading the contract.

The story was sad but all too true. It's been happening since the beginnings of recordings. The musical trio was allegedly getting ripped off.

Ladies you've got to know what is in it for you. You've first got to get to the table with a fair and honest contract. After that, you must get the contract signed as soon as possible.

Living with a man indefinitely will never get you what's entitled to you.

I believe every woman that is breaking off desserts for a man is entitled to more than being a waitress of sweets.

If a man can take the time to figure out how to lay you down, he certainly can figure out a way to marry you and make a respectable woman of you.

You will never get more in life than you asked for. Considerate and sometimes calculated demands must be made.

Too many women lay down the desserts without payment.

When dining at an establishment with servers, there is an implied contract. The contract reads as such: "If I am satisfied with the service and food, I agree to pay the prices listed on the menu along with taxes and tip."

Years ago, a similar contract existed in the relationship world. The contract read: "If you mess up my daughter, I'm putting shotgun pellets in your back."

With many fathers gone from the home, women have been left to fend for themselves.

Young women must learn the games of men quickly.

The marriage contract is the most important verbal document anyone can give and/or receive. The marriage contract usually stops the games.

The contract gives you entitlement to his time, income and assets—three key areas of life.

Time is the most important asset for all humans. After all, none of us know exactly how much time we have left, unless suicide is in the plan.

Where a man spends his time shows you what type of man he is, and what his priorities are.

I've learned over the years that people do what they want to do. People get done what they want to get done.

Even the laziest person has an agenda and priorities— to do as least as possible at all times.

If a man says, "I like you. I like you a lot," and he means it from his heart. Believe me. You won't have to call his cell ten and fifteen times a day to find him. He'll let you know where he is.

The marriage contract obligates him to tell you of his whereabouts. However, if he really cares about you, he won't want you worrying all day about his safety or trust in the relationship. So that information will be easily shared.

The marriage contract also entitles you to his income inside and out of the relationship. If children are conceived while married, the government will see about support for those children.

Of course, I know about child support for single mothers. In recent years, states have begun to clamp down on runaway dads.

I'm from the era when many of our states in the country hadn't quite figured out what illegitimacy was costing them, and many fathers were allowed to roam free with no obligation.

Today, there's a great disregard for family planning. Many of the children of today's era are born with the odds stacked against them. Many are born into situations without the father's total commitment. Many are born into marriage only to have about half of those prenatal marriages end in divorce while the child or children are still in the home. Then we ask ourselves, "why are so many of our Black youth in trouble?" The trouble began before the children had the choice to make a choice.

Living with a man indefinitely has its problems also. Only eleven states and the District of Columbia recognize common law marriage. If you live in any of the other thirty-nine states that do not recognize "common law marriage," you don't have a leg to stand on should your common law spouse die, leave or whatever. How would you feel if your common law spouse died, left you with three children and you found out that the only insurance policy he had reverted to his mother because she was the only legal beneficiary? What recourse do you have? Suppose he purchased a home in his name and you helped him with the down payment and he throws you out of the home. What recourse do you have?

The marriage contract will get you recognized in court should the relationship go south by happenstance or natural occurrence.

There are unseen benefits to the marriage contract. Many times, the marriage contract will trigger the provider instinct to operate in young men.

As I mentioned earlier, I never thought of owning a home. But when my second child was on the way, I had to find larger living quarters. At that time, I was faced with a tight decision. For a few extra hundred dollars per month (that I didn't have), I could own a home rather than rent. I jumped at the risky opportunity, because we'd have three bedrooms instead of one all for a few extra hundred dollars. I never even considered the day when we'd sell the property. That house almost tripled in value. I'll never ever rent again.

So long as a man is able to stop by and tap the honey jug for honey, his thinking will not change. He will always be in playa mode. And even if he's not a playa, he'll dodge the commitment to you for as long as possible.

Ladies, get to the negotiating table as soon as possible. And when you leave the table, have the contract signed. If he doesn't want to sign the contract, he's not the man for you.

What are you going to do? Are you going to waste your prime childbearing years on him? Or to top that, will you have his children in hopes of getting the contract signed?

Don't settle for the pipe dreams. Get your contract signed.

Make the relationship move towards marriage or separation.

What's Love Got to do with it?

Most of us have heard the song released by Capitol records in 1984, *"What's love got to do with it?"* Most of us have seen Tina's 1993 biographical movie that followed.

When the song was released in 1984, I thought it was a great song. However, after watching her biographical account on the big screen, I understood exactly why the song was written.

Let's face it, most of us, when we are young, have no idea what "love" is—especially if we grew up in an abusive situation.

Love is more of a position of character rather than an emotional feeling.

Some people find it easy to say, "I love you" when love is treated like an emotion.

Emotions, like hate, anger, empathy, and happiness are most times easily expressed.

In contrast, the character of real love is the position or decision that you've made on your mate's behalf. Real love says, "I love you even when I can't stand you. I love you when you are working my last nerve."

The character of love must be learned—not felt.

I can easily say, "I love you" when my hands are sweaty and my heart is racing out of control. It's easy to say, "I love you" when every thing is fresh and new and neither one of us has hurt the other.

However saying, "I love you," after you've called me a series of mother/fathers for being late for a date would be quite difficult. Can one say, "I love you" after realizing their entire relationship was based on a lie? Can I say, "I love you after you've wrecked my *Mercedes S55?* That's when "love" is character versus a feeling. I love you with your faults.

Most people live life in a bubble and cannot see beyond its membrane.

Our perceptions of love are based on what we've seen while growing up in our bubble.

When we're born into our families, we have no idea what it's like to be a member of the family down the street. That's a different world. Even if we were to spend a few weeks with the family down the street, we'd probably have a better grasp of the family dynamics (like—is it peace time or war time in that home—do they have general love for one another—are they raising a mass murderer), but you'd never know what it's like to be a "real" family member in the household down the street unless you decide to spend some time with them.

Plain and simple; you will not know how crazy your family is until you've observed the actions of other families.

We take our family experiences (good and bad) from dad, mom, brother(s), sister(s) and extended family and come up with a conclusion of what "love" is or is not.

That, right there in itself, is one of the biggest crimes committed that you can commit against yourself.

Honestly, we really don't have a clue what love is. Back when I was sixteen, I thought I knew what love was, until I found out my girl was kissing one of my "so-called" friends. Man, I was busted up over that for weeks.

Everybody grows up with bubble mentality. Bubble mentality is when you only have the past experiences from one source guiding your future.

I had it at work. When I first got my job, I learned quickly that if I gave the people their material when and where they wanted it, most of them were satisfied.

Well, when my customer's management staff changed and new core philosophies were introduced, I had a problem. My former successful way of doing business was obsolete, and I found myself headed towards the meat grinder.

That's why this statement is worth stating; love is a statement of character towards your mate. True love has nothing to do with emotional feelings.

Love is serious. So serious that it's mentioned in the Bible over two hundred times.

I like this scripture: *"No one has greater love than this, that a man lay down his life for his friends."* **John 15:13**.

Jesus saw the pain and suffering of going to the cross for our sins long before He got there. Yet, He went anyway, because He's got mad love for us.

When I think about how hopeless my sin situation was, I think on this scripture, and I'm reminded that Jesus really does love me. He loves all of us.

Jesus was a real man, and because of His love for us, or His character or love, He went to the cross anyway.

"...Love is patient, love is kind. It does not envy, it does not boast, it is not proud. It is not rude, it is not self-seeking, it is not easily angered, it keeps no records of wrongs. Love does not delight in evil but rejoices with the truth. It always protects, always trusts, always hopes, always preserves. Love never fails..." **1 Corinthians 13:1-8**

I was a teenager when I read this passage of scripture for the first time, and I thought I understood it very well. I wasn't perfect at it, but I thought I knew the dynamics of love.

I had to find out the hard way how real love functions when a man and woman are equally demonstrating the characteristics of love.

Love is patient. When someone says, "I love you," they'll have patience with you. If you can't cook a lick, want to remain a virgin or celibate until after marriage and/or want to wait before giving your total trust— to name a few—a man that really loves you will have patience and hold out for the appointed time.

Love is long-suffering, tolerant and stoical. A man that really loves you will take you with all of your idiosyncrasies—good and the not so good. He will love and/or tolerate your human qualities that do not agree with his.

Love is kind. Love is friendly, warm, affectionate, considerate, generous, thoughtful and of a gentle nature.

I consider myself a friendly person. I like to speak to people during the day. While walking through the halls of my job, I find it refreshing to say, "good morning" to at least one or two people before reaching my destination. You'd be surprised to see how many people will avoid eye contact, so they will not have to return the "good morning." What a shame. "Good morning" is the cheapest gift that you can give and receive from someone.

(If you're attracted to someone and every time you see them you must force interaction, trust me. They're not that friendly.)

When a man is really kind to you, he'll be considerate of your world and the happenings of your world. A kind man will do whatever is in his power to enhance your life.

Say, for instance, you work a full-time job and go to school at night and your twenty year old car just had a heart attack. A kind man that really loves you will assume your plight. Somehow, he'll do what ever is in his power to resolve your issue.

When a man is kind to you, all he possesses is yours, and he'll share it with you freely. Generosity is not a problem when kindness is at the core.

Love does not envy. Real love is the opposite of begrudging, jealousy, resentment and bitterness. If you are in a relationship with a man and he cannot handle the fact that other guys find you attractive, he has a bent version of love for you. If you've smashed up his car six months ago and he keeps bringing it up, do you think that is real love? (Love is forgiveness.) If he has bitterness from his childhood that's directed towards his mother and/or father, do you think he's capable of real love with you?

Love is not competitive. We are on the same team.

Love does not boast. When a man tells you, "I'm the greatest thing that has ever happened to you," it might be time to rethink your life options. I tell you the truth. This man is so full of himself that he hasn't and can't even consider you. The key word in the previous sentence is "full." If he's full of himself, there's no room for you or what you have to bring to the relationship. He's a self fulfilling entity. Suppose you need a shoulder to cry on?

The Bible says, "The two shall be one flesh," which means the two people become one operating unit. He'll have little room for you when it comes time to merge as one.

A real man is humble from his core. He knows who he is and is not. There's no need for him to shout, "I'm the man," because if he really is "THE MAN", his sound persona will always precede him.

We are all human. All humans make mistakes. None of us humans are perfect.

God is no respecter of persons. Everyone is created equal in God's eyes.

A boastful man will become a dictator over you. No man or woman has the right to be a relationship dictator while dating and certainly NOT while married.

Love is not proud. The pride discussed here is of an arrogant nature. Conceited, egotistical, bossy men fall into this category.

You'll never see the genuine characters of a man's heart when he is full of pride. It's layered beneath countless facades.

A man full of pride can be on the verge of bankruptcy and spend money that he doesn't have to take you on the first class vacation.

A man full of pride will get up, dress, and leave at the normal time for work even though he got fired two weeks ago.

A man full of pride will not seek counseling to get his mind right. Come on now. The man (your new boyfriend) grew up watching his daddy get dressed up in commando outfits. After his father was in full combat gear he'd climb up on the roof in broad daylight with his rifle in hand and be on pigeon stake out for the rest of the day. If that were your father, you'd be tempted to lie about that.

Usually, when a man is full of pride, something from his past is of a great embarrassment or shame to him. He compensates for that embarrassment with over the top behavior.

As we all know, relationships are built on trust. Honesty is the key ingredient when building trust in a relationship.

At the root of pride is dishonesty. Pride is not a lie told to someone else. The person full of pride lies to themselves daily.

I tell my children all the time, "Always be honest with your self." Of course you know, I don't condone lying in my house, lying is grounds for immediate discipline. My children need to understand the benefit of being honest—internally as well as externally.

Once a person begins to lie to themselves, they've submitted to the possibility of a destructive future event (i.e. divorce, lost of a friendship, and/or lost of a relationship with certain family members). Who wants a man with self dishonesty at his core? If he cannot ever be honest with himself, how will he ever be honest with you?

Love is not rude. Ladies, if you're dating a man or contemplating marrying a man that is nasty towards you, love does not exist in that relationship. I don't care if he's a thug, CEO or a CEO/thug. He has no right to be mean and nasty towards you. Don't tolerate it—ever!

Remember, you're the daughter of the King of Kings (creator of everything)! Even when you do the wrong things, God in His infinite mercy never yells, degrades, or slaps you around. So, why would a man (God's creation) have the right to do what God doesn't do?

Young women surprise me with their new dating rules. Peer pressure forces women to settle for less than they deserve.

Many young women are accepting behavior from men that God never ordained. And the young men use the guise of being a "Thug" as the escape goat for ill manors.

Young ladies, your method of operation in regards to young men should be, "you want me. Prove to me that you are worthy of me and my body. Commit to me and to me only. Man up."

If I were a woman of any color, the first time a guy that was trying to date me called me a "B" (female dog) that would be the last time he'd ever see me.

I walk on two legs—not four. I eat at the table seated in a chair—not from a bowl on the floor or not from the garbage can I just tipped over. I discriminately pick my mate—not any one that comes along with sperm.

(Female dogs let the male dogs mate and leave—no further input from the father but sperm.)

See, when put in that context, one can really see what being called a "B" is all about—personal degradation.

When I dated, I used the "B" word when one of my girlfriends made me mad or when they were acting really crabby. I don't think I ever said it to their faces.

I will say this. Back in the day, I used the word when I wanted to express the vileness of how she made me feel. When one of them irked me beyond return, the "B" word would fly out. Because, after the pinnacle of anger was reached, the "B" word was the only word that described the level of anger that I was at. And at that point, the girl was really worth nothing to me. That is as honest as I can be. I tell you that so you know what is behind the word.

Death and life are in the power of the tongue, and those who love it shall eat the fruit of it. **Proverbs 18:21** When a man can call you a "B," he is speaking death over you. Of course, it's not a physical death. However it's death nonetheless. The death is far more serious than physical death. The death spoken of here is a spiritual death. A man that will call you the "B" word is a murderer of your spirit. Would you share your body with a serial killer? Certainly not! Then, why would you allow the killer of your spirit to stay in relationship with you?

When a man calls you all manner of foul names, he's being rude. At the risk of repeating, love is not rude. Love is kind. Find someone that knows how to treat a lady.

I've seen a trend that probably started long before I've been on this planet. I was a victim of this manner of thinking a few times.

Why do women particularly young women desire the so-called "bad boys?" I had a problem with understanding it back then, and I *really* don't understand it today.

In my young years, I had a good job, and was on the same job for years—stability. I also earned enough pay to have a new vehicle, apartment—etc. yet; I couldn't believe that I was being diss-ed for a jobless wannabe thug momma's boy.

Thugs bring a certain element of excitement, risk and challenge to the relationship, and that's fun for a while. But the risks won't be that much fun when you're arraigned as an accessory to a crime.

All relationships need some form of risk and challenge. It's just a shame that under qualified brothers are given more than their fair share of opportunities to distribute unnecessary challenges and risks.

The so-called "bad boys" are usually rude and thoughtless. They talk to you like you're a servant. They never call until they have an urge. They never take you anywhere but to the corner store. They couldn't care less about your future. And many times their treatment for you (daughter of God) is less than adequate.

What is the purpose of being with a rude man?

Love is not self seeking. Real love is never selfish. Selfish people are so busy trying to get what they want that they have little regard for their friends, family members and/or mate desires. Selfish people are greedy and inconsiderate. Selfish people find it difficult to be faithful in relationships. Selfish people have difficulty participating in charitable endeavors—both financially and physically.

Selfish people will struggle with all of their relationships, because of their mindset—what is in it for me.

If you hook up with a selfish man, you'll find yourself raising his children by yourself while in the relationship. And after you're tired of being in the one-sided relationship, you'll find it hard to collect your child support checks.

His wide screen television will certainly come before feeding and clothing his children.

One clear indicator of selfishness on the man's behalf is him trying to get to the bedroom before he even knows how many fillings you've got in your mouth.

Love is not easily angered. Everyone gets angry. Even God gets angry. (If you didn't know that, you haven't been reading the Bible.) But fly off the handle anger is always unacceptable—especially when it becomes physical.

One thing I can say with all honesty that I've never while dating or married struck a woman out of anger. My motto was and is, "if I have to beat her to get her to cooperate, I don't need her."

Most women by nature are physically weaker than men. Of course, there are always exceptions to the rule. I've seen some women that I'd think twice about raising my fist to. I might catch one.

I can't understand what makes a man do that to a woman. What is he proving? That he is stronger than her? That he's the man? That he's the big ruler? What? What is the purpose of him beating her down?

Love keeps no records of wrong. "Honey, do you remember back in 1984? Before we got out of high school?"

"Remember what?"

"Don't play dumb. You remember that time I caught you in back of the snack stand with Slick Harry?"

"Yeah, honey I remember. You won't let me forget it."

"How could you do me like that?"

"Sebastian, it's been over twenty-two years since I kissed Slick and you haven't let me forget it for the last eighteen years of our marriage."

"You hurt me so bad."

"I'm sorry. I don't know how else to say that I'm sorry. Please forgive me."

In a real love relationship, there is no room for un-forgiveness. There is no room for someone with a notepad writing down every last time they've been wronged.

Anyone, that wants to dwell on the wrong doings of another many years after the offense has been committed, loves being stuck in time. Relationships have difficulty growing when the un-forgiveness notepad is in the room taking notes.

Each individual of the relationship will bring his or her element of mistakes to the relationship. None of us are perfect. Yes, you will make mistakes. We all make mistakes.

Having one of the parties in the relationship sitting there with a notepad—jotting down every wronged incident—will stifle growth and open the door of slow death for the relationship.

Love does not delight in evil but rejoices with the truth. Ladies can and do contribute to the demise of men in regards to the man's occupation. What am I talking about? Some women, given the opportunity to date a postal worker or a baller, will choose the baller. They'd choose the baller because of the cheddar (money) factor. Let's face it. A drug dealer or thief will have an excess of discretionary cash—way more play money than the postal worker or a garbage man.

Loving a man with distribution and/or proprietary issues—to name a couple, does not make you guiltless. Just because you're not selling drugs first hand, doesn't make you any less guilty than the man you call "boyfriend."

Part of the make-up of a man is the desire to make his woman happy. When you allow or a better word is support his efforts by spending the illegal cash, you're just as guilty as he is. Marry an honest person that makes an honest living. You'll sleep better at night.

It (love) always protects always trusts, always hopes, always preserves. Love never fails...

Love is a continual commitment to protecting, trusting, hoping, preserving and never giving up.

Loves always protects the object of affection. A man that truly loves his woman and children is willing to lay down his life in exchange for his family's safety. If you don't think that is true, tell your brother to walk up to an unknown married woman and slap her while her husband is standing there. Soon after you hear the popping noise from the two fleshes colliding, you'd better dial 911, because it's on and popping now.

Love always trusts. The element of trust is lacking in many relationships today. I believe the lack of trust in men has caused the marriage rate to decline with Caucasians and especially with Black people. Simply put, women can no longer rely or trust men to do the right things in a relationship because a long track record of being distrusting.

The distrust starts with fathers that do not exemplify trust from the beginning of the child's life.

Most relationships are doomed from the time the man puts forth his first example of distrust (i.e. fidelity, money, lies, and attitude).

That distrust provided by the man will agree with the woman's core beliefs instilled by her mother or other dominate females in her life.

"I knew I couldn't trust him. Mom was right. You can't trust a man."

The sad truth about the above statement is; trust is the risky part of a relationship that no one seeking a meaningful relationship can avoid—no total trust—no rewarding relationship. Risk and reward go hand and hand. It's next to impossible to have one without the other—no risk no reward.

I'm not telling you to cast caution to the wind and trust every man that comes along. Only time will tell if a man is truly *worthy* of your trust. And, you will not find out if he's a worthy candidate of your trust while in the bed on your back. It's too late for that.

Trust is the assurance that your man will do the right thing by you and your family. A trusting man brings his check home. A trusting man comes home long before the bars close. A trusting man makes sure you have a safe home to live in along with a safe vehicle to drive. And if he does not have the ability to provide all of these things when the relationship begins, he's striving for them with a vengeance.

I trust my wife. I trust her when she spends money. I trust her with the care of my children. I trust her with the care of our home. I trust her words. Without that trust, what would we have?

Suppose she told me she was going to work and I called her job only to find out she hasn't been to work in two days. Supposed after I called her job, I drove down the street and saw her car parked in a motel's parking lot? What would that do to my trust?

You can't have a loving relationship without trust.

If your man disregarded trust at anytime in the relationship, you have to reassess his trustworthiness to you, or better yet you might have to reassess the relationship.

Love always hopes. In true love, there's a drive or determination to succeed in that loving relationship.

When in relationships, always look for the "we can make it" or we can work it out" mentality—ride or die. This mindset must be equally distributed in both parties for the relationship to survive life.

I love life. At one time in my life, I didn't want to continue on the top side of the earth. Why not? Living life can sometimes suck the life out of you.

Dig real deep inside yourself and find hope. Real hope breeds determination. And the fruit of determination is success.

Ladies, when you meet a man and after the passing of time he says, "I love you" remember what love looks like. Anything less than what was previously stated in this chapter is not love.

The Bottom Line

Here is the situation, ladies. If you desire to marry, you don't have as much time as you think you do. I say that not to cause panic. I say that not for you to live a life worrying about marriage and plotting desperate ways to get down the aisle.

If marriage is one of your goals for life, don't wait until you're in you mid to late twenties to begin to plan for it. You must plan for marriage as soon as possible. Otherwise, you'll be left out.

Many single Black women over the age of thirty never realized that they'd be unwed at that stage of life. The truth of the matter is the women assumed that when it came time to marry, a man would be available. That's a good assumption if the men they desired to marry were on the same page. Many of the men are not on the same page.

Countless women have crossed the ages of thirty, thirty-five and even forty and realized that only small selections of available men are candidates to marry. Some of the men have wasted much of their lives in the prison system. Some of the men have decided that another man suits them better than a woman. Some men are on the fence—women and men, and they aren't telling anyone. And the final batch of available men (good men included) have so many circumstances of life (baby's momma, no education, no or inadequate employment, divorced multiple times, etc.) that the women realize that they are better off by themselves.

It is a shame to say it, but many of the women that cross the marrying age find themselves acting like men. Since no real candidates are available for marriage, some of the women elect to have just a good sex partner stop by, take care of business and go about his business. Is that really good for your soul and body?

God never intended for women to act like men.

And what is really sad about women acting like men is real men still want a lady. The more you act like a man, the less desirable you become as wife material. We will treat you like the man that you desire to be.

Here's the bottom line. If marriage is part of your life's plan, it must be accomplished sooner rather than later. As you move forward in life, your odds of successfully marrying diminish quickly.

I'd start plotting around the ages of 16 to 18. I know that seems early, but you don't want to be the odd woman left out. I'd make sure that all my peers knew that I respected myself and wasn't about to let anyone disrespect me. Even though it is easier said than done, I'd keep my legs closed. Sex feels good and is great, but today in 2007, having sex with too many people is like pointing a loaded gun to your head. Also, I wouldn't want to have someone else's children making me less of a candidate for marriage. I know your saying it wouldn't be easy because my friends would make fun of me, but I would remain a virgin until the man I married took me.

The next thing I'd do is to make sure that several of my daily activities took me to where the boys were—not just any boys—the boys that are "good stock." For instance, I'd go to college to educate myself. While in college, I'd take a couple of classes that had a high concentration of men. Or if I didn't aspire to go to college, I'd go to a unisex technical school that had a high concentration of skills offered to men like Heating, Ventilation & A/C, Electrical, Plumbing, etc. I'd find a man that already has the desire to educate himself.

I once read a story about a girl in the "*Millionaire Mind.*" All her life she desired to meet and marry a doctor. She enrolled in a pre-med school. After a few weeks, she started dating this guy from class. As it happened, the professor inquired about her because she had been missing from class for weeks. One of her friends told the professor that she would not return to class because she accomplished her goal—marrying a doctor. I wouldn't recommend going to school just to meet a man and then quit right after, however I do recommend going to school with a second agenda—finding a spouse. That is where most married people meet—in school first and second at work.

I wouldn't believe the lie, "you need to live a little before getting married." Yes you need to live a little before getting married, but that shouldn't include you running around sharing your body with any male with genitalia. Get your own place and transportation. Also, I'd say travel. Do something off the beaten path. Try to experience all that life has to offer before settling down. But keep the sacred things sacred. Treat your body with respect. The real truth is you do not have to share your body with anyone that you don't want to. Don't believe societies tales or fabrications.

I'm sure that eventually, the Right man will come along. After you've met someone of marriage potential, stick to the plan laid out earlier in this book.

Upon meeting a potential candidate for marriage, you always want his prevailing thought to be, "there is something about you." And the key to a successful marriage is for him to want to spend the rest of his life trying to figure out what that "something" is.

God Bless!